COTUM – Catalog of the Universal Mind
PO Box 8755
Boise, ID 83707
USA

ISBN: 978-0-578-02457-8

Front cover illustration "Saint Wolfgang and the Devil" c. 1483 by Michael Pacher, a panel of his "Father of the Church" altarpiece.

First paperback printing: May 2009

Printed in the U.S.A.

MAGIC

HISTORY / THEORY / PRACTICE

DR. ERNST SCHERTEL

ANNOTATED BY ADOLF HITLER

TRANSLATED BY COTUM RESEARCH STAFF

EDITED AND INTRODUCED BY J.H. KELLEY

ISBN: 978-0-578-02457-8

TABLE OF CONTENTS

INTRODUCTION

In May 2003, *The Atlantic Monthly* carried an article entitled "Hitler's Forgotten Library" by Timothy Ryback, author of "Hitler's Private Library: The Books That Shaped His Life." The article described various books in the library and mentioned that one of the most heavily-marked books was a strange volume by Dr. Ernst Schertel called "Magic: History, Theory, and Practice."

"He who does not have demonic seeds within him will never give birth to a new world," - that was the only example of Adolf Hitler's annotations from *Magic* that Mr. Ryback made mention of. For decades the debate has raged as to what degree the occult influenced Hitler. The annotations in the book seemed to represent the first direct link between Hitler and occult beliefs.

My curiosity got the better of me and desiring to further study what had so entranced Hitler, I searched the Internet for a translation of Magic – only to find nothing. The result of my frustration is what you're holding in your hands at this time. After several years various translators have come and gone, some holding the book for months and accomplishing nothing, while others translated just enough to figure out they found the subject matter too disturbing to continue. Now finally there is a complete translation for others to enjoy.

In my study of Dr. Ernst Schertel (June 20, 1884 – January 30, 1958) I found that he can only be described as a researcher of the unusual. After obtaining his doctorate in 1911 and graduating *magna cum laude* he authored several books focusing on dance, the occult, nudism, sadomasochism, and other topics that few dared to touch. In 1923 he authored *Magic* and sent a dedicated copy to Hitler (page 54).

In 1933 he fled to Paris after the takeover of Germany by the National Socialists, but he returned to Germany in 1934. Shortly thereafter he was rewarded with a seven year prison sentence for "spreading licentious writings." 1937 saw the revocation of his doctorate by the University of Jena. After the war he found work as an editor and proofreader, occasionally publishing his own works.

Hitler's extensive markings (sixty-six in all) in his copy of *Magic* were in the form of vertical lines in the margins. Previous reports of handwritten notes are incorrect. For ease of publication the markings have been reproduced throughout the English edition in boldface type.

I would like to thank Mr. Ryback for his *Atlantic Monthly* article, without which this project would have never been conceived. I'd also like to thank the employees at the John Hay Library of Brown University for their assistance in obtaining the Hitler copy of *Magic* on microfilm so the annotations could be reproduced.

It is my hope that the reader will find this work as fascinating as I have. I believe it gives us a new look into the mind of one of the most notorious leaders to ever exist.

JHK

PREFACE

The interest in occult problems begins today in those circles which, up until now, have knowingly, intentionally, and somewhat correctly kept it at bay. Common popular occultism exhibits certain aspects from which serious and clear-thinking men must recoil, since the entire state of our theories about natural science and awareness were not broad enough to generally allow us to deal with the phenomena of the occult.

Today's modern man of science cannot abandon his established and thorough methodology and exchange it for an, at best, dubious and gratuitously emerging "credo quia absurdum est." He concentrates instead on the exact transcribed field of any specialized science.

Such specialized science is how occultism of our time came to be. Today one can occupy himself with telekinetic experiments just as one once analyzed the laws of gravity. A number of reputable researchers found the avenue to the occult world of apparitions in this way.

With that they still did not exhaust the matter. The problem of occultism throughout the field of experimental natural sciences became so great that they moved en masse to a new, total position against it. And here the problem of occultism flows into the problems of our entire modern culture, our science, and our lifestyle.

This is the biggest reason that today – unlike more than twenty years ago – a person of understanding can no longer pass by the phenomena of the occult.

It is still necessary to count the signs which suggest that our culture is getting ready to attack its own roots. Thankfully it is essentially easy to grasp this fact of the field of exact science. Every step that has gone forward is like the blow of an axe against the supporting pillar. **A complete and new concept of truth is produced, and with that, a complete and new concept of understanding. The more exact we are in our thinking the more we open our eyes** to the vagueness of the basics of our thoughts. But it is precisely this exactness of thought that leads to the construction of an ideal world, in which the phenomena of the occult cannot only be casually questioned, but rather must be downright challenged at the theoretical level were it not already discovered. It is like the existence of the planet Neptune theoretically being found before an astronomer directed his telescope at it.

This book pursues the main points of these lines of thought. It is – in its theoretical parts at least – a theoretic awareness of nature and it practices criticism of the sum of our ideal world, in order to lay the groundwork for a new approach to things and to attain and understand our own "self." The dispute of this poses a problem, and therefore becomes a dilemma for those who are fruitful, for they believe they have reason to reject practical occultist activity

It may appear strange in our time of such intellectualism how the body is allotted such a fundamental significance, and that everything that is sensuous and animalistic appears to be assessed positively. This is one source, but it is necessary for the book to be the primary source to validate the exact profound knowledge of that which is phenomenal and that which is **irrational.** **The idea that the avenue to the last reality is found through the body and the sinking into a purely carnal form, rather than through intellect and abstraction, signifies the main antithesis** in which stands the accomplishment of our principles of commonly accepted occultism. Only through these thoughts can we begin to touch upon the explanation using the outlook of the most ancient times, those times when occultism was not merely an experimental natural science, but rather a sacred Magic and a standard criterion depicted as such, as we might, in a sense today call "religion."

At its roots, the present work represents nothing less than the immersion into an ethno-religious idea in a modern scientific form/theoretic-awareness and the stated practical achievement signifies the renewal of the lost cultic actualities of an early people.

This characteristic may just be the most difficult point, and this book allows these so-called "modern scholars" to understand it. The potential gains here get larger as soon as the reader comes to find a new position and the cardinal thoughts are thus grasped. **What is to be demanded of us is not easy, for it is to move backward to the origin of everything, a real reversal to the zenith of our culture, a recovery of that which is lost and left aside by our late-coming and familiar phrases of thoughts and experiences.**

dem Gesamtsinn des ganzen Satzes, ja des ganzen Buches abhängt.

Keine unserer Vorstellungen, ob «Imagination» oder «Wahrnehmung» kann mit irgendeinem «Ding» identifiziert werden, da Bewußtseinstatsachen nicht von «Dingen» herrühren, sondern Stoff möglicher «Dinge» sind. Es kann also an sich betrachtet auch keine Vorstellung als «wahr» oder «falsch», als «richtig» oder «unrichtig», als «wirklich» oder «scheinhaft» bezeichnet werden, da all diese Begriffe immer eine Dingwelt jenseits unserer Vorstellung voraussetzen. Ob eine Vorstellung «wahr» oder «falsch» sei, ist letztendlich nur eine Intensitätsfrage. Es gibt eben Vorstellungen, die bis zu dinglicher Intensität gelangen, und andere, die in einer matten Scheinhaftigkeit stecken bleiben. Auch hier müssen wir C. L. S c h l e i c h zitieren: «Alles Geistige, ob falsch, ob richtig, infiziert, wie die Bazillen, es übersteigert den Rhythmus des Gedankens kontaktartig; daher haben Gedanken ihre große Macht über die Massen gewonnen. Ideen sind infektiös und von der Phantasie des einzelnen gewonnene unwiderlegliche Betrachtungsspannungen, Konzentrationen des Geistes zu explosionsartigem, dynamitähnlichem Gefüge können zu der geballten Flocke werden, die durch Vogeltritt im Schnee entstanden, schließlich zur Lawine wird.»

Diejenigen Vorstellungen, welche den besten Nährboden innerhalb einer gegebenen Bewußtseinswelt finden und die höchste Intensität entfalten, setzen sich durch und gelten dann als «wahr». Auch der aufgeklärte Europäer von heute lebt zu dreiviertel von Imaginationen. Die großen Kulturen der Vergangen=

Page 63 of the Hitler copy - an example of the annotations made.

HISTORY

When nature, after millions of years of working and weaving by means of stone, plant, and animal lifted man out of her melting pot, she had created something that very well could count as the focal point of the infinite cosmic dynamic, but at the time stood only for a tiny part of the whole cosmos.

The man of primeval times felt small compared to nature and its creations. In all things and appearances, in mountains, clouds, rivers, in the world of the stars, in the fire, in the smoke, in the blowing of the wind, in the descending lightning, he recognized and admired forces and powers which were darkly related to him but still stood above him. He still had a distinct knowledge that forces of the deep filled with eerie significance were also active in the bodies of pre-human creatures: a tree, an herb, an elephant, a bull, and even a toad.

Through all of this came those peculiar processes and conditions we today call *illusions*, *hallucinations*, *delusions*, *suggestions*, *dreams* etc., which revealed to him a world of shaping strengths that are virtually hidden from present man. The man of primeval times, sleeping and awake, felt himself surrounded by a reality of images that was pregnant by a dark, often times gruesome meaning, and alive with mysterious powers. Even after he had learned to somehow control these powers and make them subservient, the feeling of eeriness and evil did not vanish, and he still stood before these things with that strange mix of feeling of superiority and fear - like an animal tamer before his beasts.

We ourselves know little about the essence of natural things, about the inner being of animals, plants, and stones, and it is not impossible that they in a - for us unapproachable - world receive and perform similar forces, like man in his world. We always adhere to the "conscious" calculation and design and in doing so overlook that the best, even in all "consciousness," always lies in the "unconscious." But we have to perceive the unconscious force of design and efficacy of natural things as tremendous, since from it originates the whole creation and our own self. The experience of this fact manifests in the rest of shock by "nature" as is still present in a sentimental form in the modern "nature-feeling."

Also animals, plants, and stones express force effects which go far beyond what is immediately obvious to our senses and can therefore very well be called "extrasensory." The ethnologist Weule wrote on this matter: "To the primitive the animal is itself something particularly mystic, with which he is also continually occupied. The animal itself performs magic, because in it there is a magic force. Often times it is even stronger than man. Of course those animals which are huntable do not come into question, but the strong and dangerous ones, and those which are on top seem eerie because of their way of living. Every tour through a larger ethnographic museum teaches just how widespread this point of view has to be." But it isn't only the animal, but also the plant and mineral unfold magic forces that can be dangerous to man, but which can, under the right circumstances, be adequately mastered into subservience.

All mastery is based on acquirement, absorption, compression, control, and design by way of subjugating the alien being to a new form-law, imbibing it to ones own world, just like the **body assimilates food. All fight for power is therefore a fight of hostile structures. Form is not dead, superficial, or unsubstantial, but the carrier of force, a mystical something that manifests itself in the proper sense of the image-laws.**

For early man there could not have been a difference between "living" and "dead" things, or even between "imaginary" and "real," instead for him there was only a hierarchy of forms, an order of images and signs in accordance with their force. For him there were visible, audible, tangible, smell-able, taste-able essentialities which have been partly there or had to be created by him and which he learned to pit against each other according to his will.

Early on he had viewed into the "continuity," into the tremendous, unbroken connection of all things cosmic, and so he knew that the smallest causes were able to trigger the biggest consequences and that even the least impressive was not without relevance.

He who knew of the secret forms, things, images, and signs was able to design forms and things, images and signs, the means to subjugate them to his law and so to dominate the universe. All that is formed is the center of forces which are in connection with the whole cosmos. Images and signs are junctions in the dynamics of the world. Things are nothing different than force focuses of the universe, just like man himself, and like every animal, every plant, every stone.

The forces of the form-world don't exhaust themselves in their crude apparent effects (which today we would call "physical" or "empirical"), instead they manifest in an unfathomable, mysterious way that is precisely called "magical" and which constitutes the last and darkest complication of the so-called law of nature, which is known to us but still partly unknown.

Early man had already coined a name for the ability of magical force to affect things: he speaks of "mana," which indwells the things and unfolds its effects according to a certain law.

The "mana" clings to the form. With its form any object, any sound, any sign is a carrier of mana. With the replication of a thing its mana is also transferred, that means the replication is loaded with the same mana as the original.

Form is always inseparable from space and time, the elements of corporeality. Space and time are the prime matter of all that is formed. So a certain point in space, a certain moment in time can be gifted with mana even if it is not immediately noticeable. Exactly because the mana force is not readily noticeable, such "abstract" carriers of mana have to be marked artificially, to in a way avoid "magical accidents," for example if someone - because of carelessness - comes close to a point which does not match the mana of the moment. It is helpful to mark such a point with the piling of sticks, with a fence or something similar, and to exactly note the time and to write the mana of every moment, every hour, every month, etc. down. The whole calendar originally had a magical foundation.

Something else comes to this: the artificial, arbitrary transfer of mana to any things, points in space, or periods of time. We call this "malediction" or "consecration." In such a case any kind of object is declared loaded with mana by the use of a spell of power. Or a square or another kind of circle is drawn on the ground with a prick, a hack, etc. and this area is then seen as afflicted with mana. The same is possible with periods of time, just as still today any day is set as a "holiday" officially. Holidays have originally been always magical times. That is why no one was allowed to work, since work always means something profane. A magical time always had to bring mischief to any activity that did not harmonise with it. Everything "magical" was at the same time also exceedingly "dangerous."

Arguably all things are initially afflicted with mana, but not to the same degree and in the same direction. In some things the mana can be so weak that it does not come into question for practical use, in other things it can reach a high degree but be so one-sided that it is ineffective in all directions. The mana of a certain place, for example, can express that only no blood is to be shed there, but it can be neutral in every other aspect.

Despite all things having mana, there will always be only a certain number of things which contain this mana in its highest intensity and with a multi-directional effectiveness, and from this fact early on came the distinction between "magical" and "profane" things. Arguably in itself everything is magical and in itself also everything can attain the highest level of magical effectiveness, but for practical purposes the aforementioned difference persists.

The magical things, that means, those which are gifted with mana in great measure, are considered to be "taboo," that means "eerie-holy." They are worshipped as "demonic."

Of course these demonic things, which represent the most tremendous focus of force in the universe, play a central role in the existence of early man. To deal with them, make them subservient, or avoid their potentially damaging effects is his most important task.

Soon in this way a magical "science" and "technique" developed, which is with its main features part of the possession of every folk-comrade (just like cookery, gardening, animal husbandry, etc.), but which is naturally in its heights and its entirety only available to a few, who then play the chosen role of the "magician" in the narrow sense of the word. The offspring for such magicians is created by means of artificial selection, so that the caste of the magicians more and more segregates itself from the profane crowd and either recruits its offspring entirely from their ranks or picks new individuals from outside their ranks according to their abilities. Very soon their suitability as magicians arises as a result of certain indicators and the inborn abilities of the neophyte are increased with the appropriate education, fertilised and lead to their maximum perfection.

Las Casas reports, for example: The Piaches (magicians) of the red Indians from Cumana select from 12-15 year old boys those which have the natural indications to be the most qualified and ablest to be educated in the art of magic. The chosen ones are sent to marked locations in the lonely forests, where some very old Piaches live and where the young people are disciplined for two years similar to a school." And so a complete isolation is obtained, to achieve the most complete disentanglement from profane surroundings and concentrate the forces. Alfred Lehmann tells about the inauguration ceremony of the Winebagos in North America: "The inauguration ceremony of the new medicine men is called the medicine celebration and is a very old institution, which like most of their celebrations consists almost entirely of dancing. The participating members form a community for themselves and have certain secrets which are never disclosed to non-members. The celebration is held in a specially arranged hut. There the members sitting at both of the long sides. The middle of the room is empty to give space for the dancers. The new candidates have to fast three days before their inauguration. In the meantime they are led to a secret place by the old medicine man that oversees the celebration and discloses all the mysteries of the society. During the fast they also undergo a rigorous sweating cure where they are covered with carpets and are exposed to the fumes of certain roots. After this is overcome the celebrations begin. They consist of dance and speeches of the old medicine men as well as of a lot of strange activities."

"Crata Repoa," an anonymous scripture from the year 1785, reports about the inauguration ceremonies of the Egyptian priests: "When someone fancied joining the society of Crata Repoa, he had to be strongly endorsed first by someone who was already inaugurated. Generally this was done by the king himself by writing to the priests. But the priests at first rejected the proposal in Heliopolis and directed him to the teachers of Memphis. From Memphis he was directed to Theben. Finally he would be circumcised. Next, certain foods were prohibited and he was not allowed to drink wine any more, until the time he reached a higher rank where he, at times, was granted permission. Then he had to live many months in an underground cave, similar to a prisoner alone with his thoughts. They granted permission to write his thoughts down, which would be thoroughly examined to become acquainted with the mind of the new member. Afterwards he was let in a hallway with Mercurial statues whereupon spells of mores were written which he had to memorize. As soon as he knew them by heart Thesmosphoros (the introducer) came to him. In his hands he had a strong whip to stop the mob at the gate of the profane, where he allowed the soon to be inaugurated new member, the eyes of whom were blindfolded and his hands were enchained with a strong linen bandage."

These examples will suffice to show the great exclusiveness of the magician caste. Only after long and exhausting inauguration ceremonies is admission granted. Because of this intricateness many who were only driven by a volatile curiosity were discouraged. At the same time it is proved during these measures if the apprentice has the necessary abilities in his body and his soul, and these abilities – if existent – will of course be greatly scattered by these sharp curves.

A great amount of irritability is a prerequisite for being granted permission into the circle of the magicians. Added to this are a lot of mannerisms and oddities which we today can still find frequently in people of "genius." Also an epileptic characteristic is considered to be a sign of magical giftedness. In any case we recognize that the magician in former times had a lot of features which we would today call "psychopathic." Today we associate with this term a derogatory meaning and do not think that most of the great things were created by these kinds of "psychopaths." Also the magician of the early times despite his abnormal predisposition should not to be pictured as an "ill" human in our sense of the word. To the contrary he had to be equipped with a great amount of robustness to be able to put up with the pathological sides of his being without impairment of his organism as a whole and to match up to all the stress that his function required. Frequently these magicians have been epic warlords who took an active part in battle and were, because of their efficiency in war, a light unto all others.

We know of the patriarch Abraham, who was undoubtedly magically gifted, that he led a very warlike life and was not afraid of any potentate on earth, and even Mohammed who was after all part of a comparatively late time period was a notable commander despite his notorious epilepsy. Also we have to visualize Moses as an imposingly coarse person despite his somnambulistic dream-story, since he would otherwise not have been able to lead a grumbling people from Egypt to Jordan with all the exertions and hardships involved. Ignatius of Loyola, who was profoundly hallucinatory-inclined and the founder of the Jesuit Order, was an outstanding soldier and a rough daredevil before he turned towards his spiritual activity. The Holy Therese (to also name a magician) was often in a state of catalepsy for days before she again began extensive organizational work which demanded high standards of her mental and physical strength.

The professional magician had the task to use his art everywhere where particularly difficult, important, or holy things were involved. But everywhere else, where the common man used magic so to speak for his domestic purposes, the individual himself performed it, similar to today, where we only take medical advice in serious cases, but treat minor cases with the use of widely known domestic remedies.   Usually the housefather or an elderly member of the extended family is the person who owns the magic recipes and has the authority to perform the required ceremonies, because not every person is able to and allowed to perform every kind of magic, even if he knows the handles, formulas, etc. that are involved.

Magic is always dangerous, is always a trial of strength between the one who performs the magic and the forces he invokes, that is to say the demonic things or simply the "demons." Out of this distinctive feature of struggle originates the aristocratic characteristic, which from the beginning was part of all magic and despite its comprehensive human basis hallmarked it as the privilege of a selected few.

The magical type of man was the one who dominated and defined all primeval cultures. The magician was in all early times identical with the "ruler," be it as chieftain or as priest or as both combined in one. He acts as intermediary between the profane reality and the world above, he himself radiates forces which exceed the normal, he is in reality the superior and the highest and so it is natural that he also holds worldly power in his hands. Even later on by the time the worldly power usually cuts itself off from the spiritual, it is still the magician, the priest who represents supreme authority and before whom also princes and kings have to bow. But not until the end of civilization, by the time the connection to the world above diminishes more and more, does the magician step back from his dominating position, the hierarchical structure of the people disintegrates, and with regard to every supernal thing every individual has to start completely from scratch.

The gruesome, otherworldly bringing to life of natural things, which is the basis of all magic, produces the world view that is known to us from so-called primitives as "animism," "pan-animism," or as "inspiriting of nature," "pan-psychical." For the primordial man "things" are dark-vivid essentialities, everything is surrounded by a holy horror which itself signifies a source for forces by which magical effects become possible in the first place. This early animism should not be confused with "pantheism" of later time periods, because animism is something that is entirely specific, is really "polytheism," but not lukewarm monotheism, which directly precedes the complete disappearance of god or gods.

Animism shows early on – in contrast to pantheism – a distinct tendency to compression, to concentration, or concretization of the demonic, just as we have also already learned with regard to mana, that is to say certain things are considered to be outstandingly demonic, whereas the demonic nature of the remaining things sinks to a harmless and therefore profane level. Since the beginning there also existed a distinct tendency to individualisation, that is to say certain people feel allocated to certain demons, family-demons and tribal-demons come into existence, in certain circumstances even pure individual-demons, which are only worshiped by one man. Alfred Lehman reports on the Negroes from the coast of Guinea: "Once some one of them decides to carry out something important, the first thing he does is to search for a god to help him in his endeavour. With this in mind he goes out and declares the first living creature that appears to be a god – a dog, a cat, or even one of the most primitive animals. Also a non-living object that he finds on his way is possible – a stone, a piece of wood or whatever else it is at that moment. He then immediately makes a sacrifice for this new god, explains his endeavour to him and vows that he will recognize and worship him as his god in the future if his endeavour succeeds." This report brings to light how closely magic is in its essence connected with animism and demonism and how far apart it is from the play we can find in atheistic "theosophy" which has a wishing-force that is only intellectual.

The magic act itself signifies a very concrete anticipation, an obvious ceremony, and beforehand acts are performed to obtain what one demands from the demon. If, for example, one wants to have rain, an act is then performed that has a distant similarity to rain, if one wants to destroy enemies war dances are arranged, if one wants to take possession of something the act of taking, stealing, or robbing is imitated, etc. Often times the ceremony can differ so much from the "natural" act that it is hardly possible for outsiders to identify both. Most often a symbol is present that is only by (indirect) way of complicated and often times arbitrary appearing associations connected to the natural image of the pertaining act.

One could say that all magic was originally based on a kind of more or less stylized "pantomime," that is to say based on a part theatrical and part dancing presentation of what one wants to accomplish. This brings to light the magic origins of all ceremonial arts. But dance also plays from another point of view a big role in the old magic - namely as a creator of manic conditions and as a means to work off states of tension. There have been and there still are dances which serve the purpose to artificially create states of "ecstasy" or "possession," where the dancing person feels imbued with the god and with this demonic completeness of power exerts magic effects. In this case the dance directly creates the demonization, but at the same time also serves as an outlet, that is to say by means of abreaction. This kind of dance expresses convulsive, paroxysmal strains of the body and at the beginning wants nothing less than to be "lovely."   Their purpose is only to create a frenzy which will be facilitated by all kinds of other means, such as excessive fasting, sweating, flagellations, glaring light effects and sounds, as well as narcotic beverages and smoking.

Alfred Lehmann brings a report about these "magic dances," wherein such a ceremony which is commonly practiced by the Tunguses is described: "In the middle of the yurt (hut) flickered a bright fire around which a circle of black sheepskins were laid, on which a shaman was loudly reciting incantations and going around with well measured and tactful steps. His garb was a long gown made of fur, whereupon straps, amulets, chains, bells, and pieces of iron and copper were hanging from top to bottom. In his right hand he had a magic drum formed like a tambourine that was likewise decorated with bells and in his left hand he had a bow. His look was dreadfully wild and terrifying. The assembly sat quietly, but with the most expectant alertness. Gradually the flame in the middle of the yurt went out; only the coals still smoldered and spread a mystic twilight. The shaman threw himself to the ground and after lying there for about five minutes he started to moan woefully, a kind of hollow or suppressed screaming, which sounded like it came from different voices. After a while the fire was again blown on and it blazed away high into the room. The shaman leaped up, put his bow on the ground and by holding it with his hand and placing his forehead on the upper end of it, he began – at first slowly, then gradually faster, to run around the bow in a circle. After a good while of spinning he suddenly stood still without any sign of dizziness and with his hands began to describe figures in the air. Then in a kind of excitement he gripped his drum, which he stirred with a certain melody, after which he soon jumped around sometimes faster, sometimes slower, while his whole body twitched here and there unbelievably fast in a peculiar manner. During all these operations the shaman had, with a certain craving, smoked a few pipes of the most aggressive tobacco and between each one of them drunk a gulp of brandy. Suddenly he fell on the ground and laid there frozen and lifeless. Two of the attendants lifted him up and placed him upright on his feet. He looked ghastly. The eyes stood wide and vacant out of his head, his whole face was red all over, he seemed to be in complete unconsciousness, and except a slight shudder of his whole body there was no movement at all for a few minutes, no sign of life was noticeable. Eventually he seemed to wake up from his stiffness. With the right hand based on his bow, he quickly wielded the magic drum with his left hand and, jingling it around his head, then put it down to signify that he is now totally excited and that one could now ask him questions. His answers to these questions were given without long reflection, but in such a way as if he himself did not know what was going on."

In this case we have to interpret the dance movement as an ecstatic and demonic moment, which in combination with narcotic means (nicotine and alcohol) produces a state of "possession" (trance, somnambulism), in which an extensive shifting of the "ego" happens, so that apparently someone else (a "ghost") speaks out of the pertaining body.

Dancing is also a central part during a magic healing ceremony, which Alfred Lehmann mentions from some red Indian tribes, at the beginning it is in the form of a pantomimic ceremony, but it gradually leads to ecstasy. It says: "The dance is literally a performance which the medicine man performs at the sick bed before an awe-struck audience. Beating on a small drum or banging with a rattle, he moves in a circle and states that he is conversing in a mythical way with the ghosts, sucks the sickness out of the patient's stomach or neck, chases bad ghosts out of various parts of the body, etc. Continuing in this way he not only brings himself but also his audience and patients into a state of ecstasy, wherein those same patients stare at him with fear and tremor. And when he shakes his magic rattle or beats his small tambourine they imagine that heaven and earth are listening and that the whole universe bows before him."

J.W. Hauer writes about dance as a means to the ecstatic: "That the dance is primarily a means of amusement is a false delusion, as the comparing ethnography shows. For the red Indians of Tarahumara, for example, the only big sin is to not dance enough, and according to Preusch dancing is a very serious matter, comparable to a kind of prayer or magic rather than an amusement. Indra, the god of battles and weather, surely did not dance for amusement; likewise with Marut. Indra's dances must have a deeper meaning. They are strength-stirring and life-creating. But the strength-effecting dance is at the same time also an ecstatic dance. In Indra's case the dance is connected with manifestations of strength. This will suffice to show that Indra's dances are indeed wild and ecstatic ones."

We are always inclined to dismiss everything that is associated with ecstasy, somnambulism etc. as belonging to the area of "empty imagination," as "lacking scientific insight" or even as "sickly," and believe to **settle the affair with this classification. But we don't take into consideration that our norms of "reality" and "imagination," of "true" and "untrue," of "healthy" and "sick" are indeed relative and that there can be conditions of the soul where these concepts** literally turn around, and where we cannot simply reject these conditions of the soul as unjustified. Just as there is not only one but infinite "geometries," which are completely coherent and reasonable, so are there infinite possibilities of a world view and a resulting attitude, which, despite contradicting each other, exist in themselves with complete justification and could never in the sense of a line of argument be pitted against each other.

We already indicated that the type of the "magical man" does definitely not signify something "ill" in the common sense, despite displaying a lot of symptoms which we call "pathological" in our world sphere. In his sphere the magician operates indeed as "healthy" and shows the essential attributes of the "healthy," that is to say courage, self-confidence, ability to cope with life, etc. Likewise there appears what we call "imagination" completely as reality in their associated world and our "realities" appear there simply as obtuse imbecilities quite frequently.

Since all magic is in one way or another based on animism and demonism – contrary, for example, to our empirical domination of nature – it is explainable that the cult of the demons is also at the fore outside of the closer area of magic. The demonic basic outlook crosses all areas of life, and since the connection with the demons is only possible in the magical way, the magical actions and thinking manifest themselves in every condition of life and in every smallest handling. The whole being is layered around a magic-demonic center and receives its purpose from there, its blessing and its strength. But this is religion. All religion is only a form of magic and all magic is only applied religion. About this writes Alfred Lehmann: "How closely cult and magic were interwoven together follows explicitly from the incantations. [Very often these are introduced with appeals to the pertaining gods, so that we would rather call them hymns, songs of praise,] if they would not explicitly be called incantations in the documents." Rudolf Utzinger also paints a vivid picture of this convergence of magic and demonic lines in the religion of the occult: "The religious privileges of the mature man are explained to the child in a tender, sensitive way, in order that it gets to know the demonic mask-dancers and the mythological vital forces since its youth and on the occasion of the Kachina celebration. The child gets well acquainted with how to beg the gods for rain, fertility, and the benedictory strength of the sun. The cult objects bear witness to a conscious symbolism in form and color. To the outsider these things: rainbows, bolts of lightning, corncobs, rain clouds, may seem dull as long as he is not able to decipher the foreign phenomenal world. Behind the language which is clear and certain in its form hides a world of pious shudder and childlike - as well as serious - mysteriousness. The contours change into luminosity of magical immersion. The figures have the reason and the obsession of magical vision. A rush for naturalness, an intuition about the emotional turmoil of another ulterior pool of light."

All concrete worship of god or gods grows out of a magical foundation. That is why early on the terms "magician" and "priest" have one and the same meaning. The magician is the servant and the representative of the deity, in a sense its tyrant, and in a state of ecstasy he is even its direct incarnation.

This is already signified in the costume, in the emblems, and in the whole manner of appearance. The magician and priest wears the attribute of his demon, in the Assyrian-Babylonian cultural sphere, for example, he wears a pyramid-shaped or conical hat which is reminiscent of the mountains of gods and the old temple towers, or he wears some kind of horned headgear which is reminiscent of the bull and ram cults. He is dressed in a long white coat, which represents a very primeval divine symbol, and in his hand he carries the rod of the ruler (rod of the magician), which is from time immemorial a symbol of the godly fertility and almightiness.

Frequently masks are directly applied to further clarify the oneness of the magician with the god.

The demonic cult consists of the performance of mystical ceremonies which refer to the character and the form of activity of the relevant demon, and consists of the making of sacrifices by which the magician connects himself and his tribe with the deity and always acquires new fullness of strength.

The sacrifice is the most mysterious fact in the whole demonic cult. The point is not only to give the demon any kind of things as "presents," to propitiate him in this manner, but its real importance is the mystical becoming-one with the demon itself. With the sacrifice the demon always gains new fullness of the blood and reality, while the acting magician and his community are saturated with new demonic strengths. For that reason alone it is obvious that magic without an explicit demonic cult is essentially not possible, because only with the cult and with the sacrifice does the demonic strength grow and magical abilities increase.

Tiele writes about the importance of the sacrifice: "The gods depend on the sacrifice and long for it. Like a bull does the god roar for the sacrifice. The god longs for the sacrifice and for its master, the almighty Brahman, the one making the sacrifice. What happens inside the sacrifice is described with quaint verbalisms and with a sometimes incomprehensible symbolism as the most important in heaven and on earth. The sacrifice gives and creates everything. In this way does the sacrificial hymn, the sacrificial formula, the Brahman obtain domineering power. The dependence of the gods on the sacrifice is even carried so far that one thinks of the god as a creation of the sacrifice. In the sacrifice lies the secret of existence, the soul of all beings, the soul of all gods. For that reason the power of the one making the sacrifice is unlimited."

The point of the sacrifice is the unification and the amalgamation with the demon and originally had very bloody and orgiastic patterns. Since initially the demon is always thought of as incarnated in a human - the oldest sacrifice is the human sacrifice, and since the sacrifice always consists of an "eating" of the sacrificed one – we clearly recognize the magical-sacred roots of what we call "cannibalism."

The intellectual of today only has a scoffing smile for these things, since from the heights of his "bodiless knowledge" he no longer recognizes the deeper connections of reality. For the old peoples the consuming of a "body" – irrespective of whether animal or human – was something gruesome-holy and of darkest magical importance. Even in the moderated religions of our time we can still see the bloody origins of individual rites.

Leo Frobenius describes a sacrificial ceremony which not long ago was still commonly practiced by the African Yoruba people on the occasion of the induction into the Ogboni secret society: "When the sacred apparatus was displayed at the initiation of a new member, those present stripped themselves to the waist. They then stepped up to the bronze effigy in the lurid light of a huge fire and greeted it in chorus with a shout of "Hecqua!" Then the first sacrifice was offered up. A human being was beheaded in such a position above the pair of Eda-Items that the blood poured over them. Occasionally, when a more important ceremony was deemed necessary, several human beings were sacrificed, and on the admission of a new member, a white and red kola nut was placed at the side of the effigy, and a second red one in human blood on the Eda-Item itself. This last nut represented the sacrificial blood which the novice had to consume with his mouth. For this purpose the candidate was blindfolded. Bending forward on his knees in front of the images sprinkled with sacred gore until his forehead touched the ground, he had to jerk himself forward, blindfolded, to the images lying on the ground. He was guided until he was prone upon the earth with the upper part off his own body lying in blood. He had to stretch his head forward until he could pick up the kola nut on the blood-dripping Eda-Item with his lips. Then he ate it. Then he returned to an upright position. The celebrating priest then took hold of each of the Eda-Item in either hand, so that the chain (by which they were connected) hung down and the ends of the figures (which were made of iron) turned towards the novice.   Holding the iron tips parallel, he first touched both of them with the corners of the candidate's mouth, then poked both of the ends of the sticks into his nostrils, and, finally, touched his forehead with them. This ritual meant to convey that the holiness absorbed by the novice in eating food steeped in human blood in a hallowed place through his mouth should also be transferred to the other parts of the body. This ceremony being concluded, the shout of "Hecqua!" was raised once more. Then a kola nut was shelled, one of its sections laid upon the breast of the female Eda-Item, removed again by the priest, broken into pieces and distributed among the people to be consumed together."

The cannibalistic foundation is still distinctly present here. But we observe that already a form of "replacement" is introduced, so that the human is not sacrificed but instead a nut soaked in his blood. A certain process of abstraction already establishes its position, which corrodes from the original bloody sacrifice to bloodless replacements.

A very abstract form which the sacrificial techniques have developed in the European cultural sphere, but still distinctly refers to the bloody foundation is, at present, in the Catholic mass. Here bread and wine are the replacements, but the consciousness, that this is the flesh and the blood of a human god, is still clearly preserved.

The following is an excerpt from the book of P. Anselm Schott, which plainly illustrates these facts: "God exerted all means of almightiness and wisdom to enhance the sacrifice of the cross and to give it everlasting importance. He made the once opened source of his lifeblood into a vast stream, which flooded the whole of God's kingdom on earth and the whole of the Holy Church. As often as a poor human, who is consecrated by the bishop as a priest, changes bread and wine into the body and blood of Jesus Christ, the sacrifice of reconciliation on Golgatha is renewed. Jesus Christ is indeed sacrificing himself on the altar, truly like on Mount Calvary. The priest elevates him, shows him to the people and by separating the body from the blood, the consecrated host from the chalice, Jesus appears as slaughtered and deceased, as the lamb whose lifeblood to the last drop has run out of its body. The word of the priest which changes and separates the forms is much like the sacrificial sword under which the lamb is slain. The breaking of the consecrated host represents the violent sacrificial death of the Lord. Heaven itself is lowered to earth, the earth is lifted to heaven, and heaven and earth are connected, reconciled, married. Encouraged and strengthened by the prayers, the priest enjoys the body and the blood of the lord."

We learned that the connection with the demonic world is the foundation of magic. But this connection happens in the sacrifice. The sacrifice creates the state of ecstasy where the human connects with the cosmic forces, so that he is able to perform magic effects. J. W. Hauer writes about this: "During the sacrifice it is above all during the enjoyment of the sacrificial potion or the sacrificial meal, that the gods participate or that their secret strength breezes, which creates such enthusiastic, heaven-assailing ecstasy, which lets all gravity of the earth vanishing in the beatific presence of the gods, who came rushing to the sacrifice with a thirsting desire, or to which the one making the sacrifice himself on the wings of the sacrifice is carried."

The more or less abstract and essentially atheistic-orientated, concentration-practices of today's Yogis, for example, aim at nothing else than the connection with the world above, to "harness" (Yoga-yoke) the para-cosmic forces, and must consequently be seen as very abstract forms of the sacrifice. It is not by accident that the old sacrificial words "Brahman" and "Om" still have a pre-eminent part today and that also the old sacrificial dances still shine through in their standing and sitting practices.

The witches during the middle-ages likewise had a magical feast and dance as the center of their cultic practices, and unification with the demonic world was carried out by them in a most palpable manner.

As soon as contact with the para-cosmos is made the different paths of magical activity come up by themselves almost automatically. Some rays of light shall be cast on these now.

The magical forces can always be directed in more diffuse or in more specialised courses, and out of this flow indefinitely various forms of magical effectiveness.

Among the diffuse forms it is especially the general determination of fate which characterises the most immediate and the most spontaneous expression of magical potency. All men of genius **possess this strength, and all peoples, whose history did not just "happen" but whose history did virtually condense into a myth, did possess it. With this diffuse determination of fate the para-cosmical (demonic) forces are without a doubt harnessed and assimilated, but they are apart from that given free reign in order that they are able to operate in an autonomous way. This can be combined with a lot of misery and misfortune but always leads to a consequence with the deepest meaning.**

A steering of the magic forces in a special direction can be seen in all of the acts, which are in the narrower sense called "enchantment." This is about the concentration of the magic force towards a certain person or any other kind of object, to create very particular magic effects. If concrete things are involved it is from time immemorial common practice to create a picture of the pertaining item, to possibly add parts of the real thing (hair, splinters, secretions, etc.) and to then carry out with this picture what one wants to have accomplished with the pertaining object itself. This is called "pictorial magic." The word "picture" has to be understood in the widest sense. These are not necessarily exact replications of the object, but every piece of wood, every kind of vague drawing in the sand and under certain circumstances the pure concrete imagination are enough. It is only crucial that something is used as a substitute for the real thing. Therefore pictorial magic comes into consideration only where the real object is difficult to access for direct magical manipulations.

"Amulet magic," in its widest sense, is in a certain way associated with pictorial magic, that is to say the creation of objects which are loaded with magic force by the use of certain acts. This kind of enchantment is also applied if the magic ceremony can not be performed at the place or at the time where the magic effect should happen. Amulets are accumulators of magic force or magic "infernal machines." Amulets and talismans already can be found among the most primitive peoples, and their creation is partly based on utilisation and skillful combination of the natural magic forces of stones, metals, and organic substances, as well as based on "speaking to" these assembled objects, whereby also the appropriate alignment of the stars, the orientation of the talismans, and much else matter. Certain magic syllables, written on little notes and added to the whole, belong to it, as do scratched or painted magical signs. Amulet magic can be steered like pictorial magic into totally opposite directions, it is able to heal and destroy, can inspire love or crush it, can give strength for battle or weakness, and much more. The difference with pictorial magic is only that the amulet must be worn by the one it is designed to have effects on, while pictorial magic is designed for the farthest distances.

"Necromancy" or conjuration of the dead is a kind of magic activity where the magician invokes a dead person to perform magical effects through him, which in many cases has reached a high degree of perfection. This kind of magic rests upon the thinking that death produces a "demonization" of the pertaining individual, so that this person does now not appear as a human any more but as an "animal," as a "ghost," or a "demon." This perception derives from the situation that "dead" things are easily sensed as a seat of demonic forces, partly because of the horrified unfamiliarity we have with all which is dead, and partly because of the switching off of the "conscious" life, whereby (like in deep sleep) a closer contact to para-cosmical forces seems possible. Therefore necromancy only represents a special kind of demon evocation, and the mortuary cult we can find with many peoples, and which is only minimally alive in our "spiritualism" of today, is only a special kind of demonic cult.

The purpose of magic procedures was not always to actively affect the environment, but frequently only to passively "listen into" or "see into" cosmical and para-cosmical connections. This is called clairaudience or clairvoyance and insofar as it is about investigations about the future it is called prophecy or soothsaying. Originally, prophecy meant just "speaking while being delighted with god," and this already shows that for this kind of magic the amalgamation with the demon, that is to say an ecstasy (trance) was seen as a precondition as much as with every other kind of magic.

The methods of prophecy are countless and they fluctuate in colourful abundance between simple clairvoyance without any kind of special direction and the most complicated instructions and techniques. These different observances have the tracing out or artificial construction of certain concentration points in common, in order to reach a state of clairvoyance. It is relatively unimportant if this concentration point rests in a crystal, a glass of water, a plate with tea leaves, an animal's liver, or in the flight path of a bird. Although all these methods are carried out on the basis of established and learnable "rules," experience shows that these rules are only "cultic rules," that is to say they are indeed individual and that the magic ability of the individual is always the one key factor. Reading the cards is also done with stringent rules that have thousands of years of tradition. Nevertheless, not every random person is able to investigate the future on the basis of these rules alone if he does not have the necessary clairvoyant abilities. Even in astrology, which is after all a virtual mathematical science, only the one who has the necessary natural magic talents alongside of his scientific-astronomical education will be able to produce satisfying results.

Until now we have explained merely a cross section of the history of magic, we have presented a morphology of magic and would now have to describe her historical development. But a history of magic cannot be written in the same manner as, for example, a history of physical science. Our knowledge of the old peoples and the exotic is insufficient to establish a "biogenesis" of its darkest, most cryptic and more or less secret beliefs and activities.

Whenever we encounter a people we find that they possess magic systems and practices, but we are often unable to ascertain how these systems emerged, where we could speak of influence, or even what justifiably should be set as "earlier" or "later." We can only speak of the "old" or of the "exotic" and have to treat a millennium as if it were a day. On the other side magic, by its nature, resists the use of our concepts of "development" since it rests too much on intuitive knowledge and autogenic power. Arguably, great magicians are replaced by mediocre ones, and times where magic dominates and penetrates all life are replaced by times where magic recedes, but true "progress" in our rationalistic sense can be demonstrated nowhere. It would instead be possible only to speak of a constant "regression." Almost everywhere we find magic forms we also find ossification and corrosion of these forms. It almost seems as if humanity in earlier times was in possession of all magical abilities and since then has only slumped from this height. How man was able to reach this high standard is completely **unknown to us. In any case all theories which speak of constant "progress" of world affairs fail here. It isn't entirely coincidental that the old religious systems of better times held the view that man does not reach salvation by "progress" but by a "conversion."**

Therefore, we can demonstrate clearly only the history of the degeneration of magic. This degeneration coincides with the gradual crystallisation of that world view and attitude which we call "European" in the widest sense. We not only mean a world sentiment which would only appear inside of Europe in its geographic or even racial meaning, but (structurally-psychologically) the form of human existence that may have reached its climax in today's Europe. The more a people converge to this "European" state, the more its magical capability wanes and conceals its magical forms of expression. But with this the ground is cut from under the whole religious life and it degenerates into bloodless, abstract theorems with atheistic tendencies.

The Europeans and with them the "late" type of man is in general characterised by his lack of feeling for the "concrete," "corporeal." He does not experience the physical world as something intrinsic and substantial, and he therefore lacks every sense for the deeper meaning of the gestalt-like, the actual. It is always said that the European has a pronounced "sense of reality" and "sense of fact." But closer inspection reveals that he always looks past "reality" and the "facts" and what he holds in his hands are empty schemes. The whole materialism and rationalism of our time virtually strikes in the face every deeper sense of reality and facts.

But magic in the proper sense is something "concrete" and therefore irrational and anti-materialistic, it works with the blood and soul of the things, images, figures, and everything which is called "body" is a source and reservoir of power. Nothing is more disastrous for the magician than abstract thoughts which slide into his quite plastic imagination during the exercise of his art, and nothing weakens the magician as much as when his brain momentarily runs dry and loses contact with the physical world.

The European type of man is solely attuned to this running dry of the brain and therefore he is not able to grasp the fullness of reality anymore. "What I don't clearly and distinctly recognize, is not" says Descartes, and this shapes the fundamental principle of European rationalism. But especially the deepest things are those which we are not able to clearly and distinctly recognize. And even if we could, still nothing would be done for the magical side of our being, since "recognising" in the rationalistic sense is always a fake and shallow understanding of the actuality, and is consequently more dissolving of the contact with forces of the deep than creating it.

The development in the direction of the European pole and therefore the degeneration of magic, of demonism, and of religion begins around the world roughly at the same time, namely about 500 years before Christ. The year 500 B.C. identifies the climax of magical consciousness. At that time, Lao Tse was working in China; a representative of a certain enlightened mystic, in India Buddha was completing Brahmanism, in Persia Zoroaster was reforming the older magic and was founding his quite rationalistically substantiated sect, which could not, except for today's "Bahai" and "Mazdaznan," deny its relationship with the specific European type of thought. In Palestine during that time the Jewish prophets were operating, who were standing in sharp contrast to the magic oriented Yahweh-cult of the old Jews and was railing against concrete divine service, in Greece finally the first "philosophers" began to appear, who have corroded the magical consciousness of early times and were helping to pave the way for European intellectualism. And if we would know more about the cultural history of America we could probably demonstrate similar developments there, too. The Spanish conquistadors were in any case reporting that they were considered to be the reincarnation of a legendary religious founder, who in a not-too-distant past fought against the magical blood-cult and hence played a similar role as the Jewish prophets.

The fading of the feeling for the corporeal, the loss of meaning for the deeper content of the concrete, the pictorial, the shaped, in short for the filled, united form, at first resulted in an abatement and abstraction of demonic perceptions. The demons were less and less conceived as fleshly-bodily and concrete, but more and more as purely mental potencies, that is to say finally diluted to purely conception-schemes. This clearly comes to light in the system of the platonic "Doctrine of Ideas."

On the other side the tendency towards abstraction did manifest itself in the direction that the concrete borders between the peoples and therefore the religious borders were perforated and a sole demon was held up as a theoretical world principle, that is to say the transition from concrete polytheism to abstract monotheism was implemented. There arguably has always been a hierarchy of the demons and one of them was always considered to be the supreme and most powerful, but this was always a different one for each people, and one would have been wary to appoint a totally shady concept as a universal-demon for all people.

This tendency which manifested itself in the generalisation, and with it in the abatement of the godly perception, is closely connected with the process of abstraction we can call "universalism." **The concrete human, the concrete people, the concrete gods are thereby eliminated and in their stead the abstract notion of "humanity" is placed, above which a likewise purely conceptual "Monotheism" is enthroned. The slogan of "humanism," of the general "humanity," the universal manhood, derives from this tendency of universalism of a late time, likewise do dreams of a "solely true world religion" and random "exhilaration of humanity," which both once again flourish today.**

The immediate consequence of abstract monotheism was the establishment of an absolute "morality," which was seen as equally applicable for all people. The early time knows no morality in this universal sense. Its rule of life is given by the folkish "custom" and by the will of the tribal god, whose governing was utterly autocratic, and was giving **orders at his discretion. These as well as the customs of the people can potentially be very violent and "immoral," they can demand blood and destruction and have nothing to do with "humaneness," "brotherly love," or an abstract "good" of some sort. The pertaining rule of life always stays limited to the individual nation and this nation conceives it as completely natural that other people again have other guidelines for their** way of life. The abstract Monotheism of recent times is just the epitome of an abstract morality, which intrudes in the most rigorous way on the whole of "humanity."

This so-called "good," for which the late universal moral strives, consists of an apotheosis of the abstract and rational and therefore of an alienation from the concrete, from the body, from the picture, from the irrational-compulsiveness. It is a moral of castration and abatement, just as abstract monotheism is appearing as an emasculated and waned demon. The fleshly-strong, aristocratic ideal of life of earlier times is forsaken and forgotten in favor of a sentimental levelling down, which seeks the imprisonment and domestication of all mankind.

But magic is something primeval, heroic, unsentimental, something violent, aristocratic, bodily-concrete, which resists every abstraction, universalism, and moralisation. Magic is the plunder of demonically imbued men.

It is therefore self-evident, especially in the late European cultural sphere, that there has been little liveability for it, and that it – **just like the heroism of early times – was condemned to decline in every place where humanistic-universalistic trends have gained the upper hand.** Its downfall would have been even faster if not for Catholicism in Europe, Hinduism in India, and in other countries where atavistic tendencies have come to its assistance.

European Catholicism, which is mainly derived from Egypt, still fosters the old traditions of the magical significance of the body, the picture, in short the concrete-designed in general. The Catholic cult was built on magical ceremonies, in its center the sacrifice was still featured like in old times, its world was still replete with demons and even the supreme God still appeared in the guise of bread and wine. Here there was still air for magic of all kinds, and it was not coincidental that with the resignation of Catholicism, magic also dried out in Europe.

The Catholics did indeed fight pagan/demonic beliefs, that is to say pagan religion and magic, but they didn't label them as "untrue" but as "satanic." Catholicism in no way denied the existence of the demons, just as it failed to deny the existence of Satan himself. Pagan magic was considered to be the work of demons. About this Lactatnius declared: "Demons are the cause of astrology, divination, the practice of augury, and of those very practices which are called oracle-giving, necromancy, magic." With this the reality of demons was fully admitted, and with the differentiation between "black" and "white" magic, which arose in the early middle ages, did pagan magic also obtain a position in Catholic dogma. Soldan extrapolates the word "black magic" from the Greek "negromancy" (black-art), but that constitutes only a malapropism of the original word "necromancy" (evocation of the dead). "Black magic" always meant pagan magic, which worked with the help of pagan gods (those "demons"), while the notion of "white magic" combined all - by the Catholic cult - permitted magical actions which were then attributed to the universal-Monotheism and his "angels." This is how it came to be that an activity of "black magic" (witchcraft etc.) was interpreted as the crime of heresy, that is to say as apostasy of the solely authorised Monotheism, but without – as during the later enlightenment - regarding it as nonsense and fantasy. The concepts of "black" and "white" magic are completely relative, and are only derived from Catholic dogma, and so it was perhaps often times hard to decide if there was a "demon" or an "angel" behind a certain magical phenomenon, since both are ultimately the same.

Since the Catholic cult itself constituted a fully developed magical system, it was natural that it also rubbed off on "black" magic, so that large parts of pagan magic now received a Catholic varnish and could, with due care, also be practiced openly. So eventually the old magic did flourish again - with the corresponding transcription – and astrology, Kabbalism, and alchemy reached remarkable climaxes.

Astrology, the art of investigating the future from the stars, is from very old Egyptian documents found as early as the 12th century B.C., which deal with "stargazing" and "day selecting." During Alexandrian times astrology experienced a tremendous boom, where it got an expansive systemic foundation from the astronomer Claudius Ptolemaeus. In connection with Greek philosophy and natural science this antique astrology then spread into the medieval European cultural sphere.

Kabbalism was fruit born from the tree of Jewish mystique and religious philosophy. "Kabbalah" means (as is was said) "tradition" or "hearsay," that is to say a system of thought which was not given directly in the Old Testament, but existed alongside it as oral tradition. The origin of this tradition was placed back by the Jews themselves to the beginning of the world, but the form of the Kaballah which got to Europe during the middle ages did not develop until around 1000 years A.D. It crossed Spain and entered Europe at the beginning of the second millennium.

Two different things about the Kabbalah have to be distinguished: First, its mystical philosophy about religion; and second, the methods by which it tried to harmonise this philosophy with the Old Testament. The doctrine of the Kabbalah was a true secret science, that is to say its knowledge was in the hands of a few rabbis and was only passed on by way of personal schooling to a carefully selected younger generation. As a living entity it often times stood diametrically opposed to the wording of the more or less frozen dogmas of the Old Testament, but at the same time meant not to negate but protect them. They helped themselves with complex manoeuvres of reinterpretation, which were expanded to very ramified and pedantic methods that almost became an end in themselves.

The Hebraic alphabet played into the hands of such letter-stunts in a desirable way, since it contained only consonants, whereas the insertion of the vowels would not be done until the normal reading of the text. In addition to this came that every alphabetic character signified a certain number (like some letters in the Roman alphabet), so that the numeric value of whole words could also be used for reinterpretation. During the middle ages this whole branch of the Kabbalah developed into an independent art of writing, arithmetic, and interpretation. And with all of its myriads of demon-names and magical seals it was almost indispensable for the whole magic of that time.

The scholastic branch of the Kabbalah matters little to us today, but the almost overgrown content of the Kabbalistic doctrines still radiates in undiminished intensity. The following short paragraph shows the beauty of this language and its magical content: "After God had created the night to let the stars shine, he turned against the shadow he had created, looked at it and gave it form. He pressed an image on the veil, wherewith he had depressed its vagueness, and this image smiled back at him. He wanted this image to be him, to form man after his likeness. He looked at this figure, which one day should be the one of man, and his heart softened, because he already believed to hear the lamentations of his creation. And god became human, to be loved and understood by the humans. The only thing we know about him is this image, which is pressed on the veil, which hides the brightness from us. The image is ours, and he wants that for us it should be his. God sits on a throne that glitters with countless sparks and he lets them grow into worlds. His hair glows and stars emerge from it. The worlds surround his head and the suns are coming to bathe in his light. The figure of god is twofold. He has a head of light and a head of darkness, a white and a black, a superior and an inferior. All light requires darkness and only becomes brightness because of darkness. The bright head trickles a dew of sweat onto the dark head. Open to me, my love, says god to man, for my head is drenched with dew, and my locks with the tears of the night. The white head is the light, but the black head is the lamp. Nothing comes from god alone. All that is appearing and disappearing appears and disappears in his shadow. But Israel separated the white head from the black head. And so gods shadow became the phantom of the devil."

The doctrine of the Kabbalah combined the angels, demons, and god together as the embodied dynamic of the universe and here it also touches on our theory of magic and demonology, which will be discussed later.

Alchemy, the most important discipline of medieval magic next to astrology and the Kabbalah, seems to have its origins in Egypt, where the "hermetical books" represent its oldest description. By intervention of the Greek atomists this ancient form of what is known today as "chemistry" reached Europe.

The basic idea of alchemy - the possibility of conversion of the substances and the creation of the one from the other - is only possible on the basis of a theory of atoms and elements, but also involves certain energetic reflections. Where to draw the border between "natural science" and "magic" is as hard to determine as the difference between chemistry and physics. That alchemy had a magical aspect follows from one of its main propositions: "If you do not take the physical state away from the objects, and if you do not reorganize the bodiless substances into bodies, then you will not achieve what you are expecting." Insofar as this does not just mean a process of gasification, this sentence has to be applied to certain transmutation-phenomena, which are so highly complex that they touch on magical phenomena.

The aim of medieval alchemy was the discovering or the synthetic production of the "philosopher's stone," a peculiar catalyst by means of which it should not only be possible to gain eternal youth and heal every kind of illness, but especially to artificially create gold from any kind of metal. From today's state of chemistry these ideas are not beyond the realms of the impossible, since the effects that radioactive matter has on the organism have been discovered and the objections which have been raised against the existence of a "primary matter" have disappeared. However, if the medieval alchemists indeed have been successful in discovering this prime matter and really performed the wonders which have been passed on about them can probably never be clarified.

Beside these forms of magic, which were permitted to a certain extent by the Catholic Church as "white," a more or less forbidden thick undergrowth was pullulating, that is to say practices which where considered "black" and which where summarized in the widest sense as "witchcraft." Witchcraft manifests itself as a degenerated and vulgarised form of elements, which originated from the sacral magic of antiquity, but did not get approbation from the Catholic Church. The nerve center of witchcraft was the artificial creation of somnambulant dream states, by using narcotic salves and inhalants modelled on antiquity, and the consequential experience of amalgamation with the otherworldly (demonic) potencies analogous to antique sexual mysteries. This devil-love actually represented only a very primeval form of "communion" with the deity, which was also sanctioned by the Catholic Church. What gives witchcraft its somewhat disgusting varnish is its low and plebeian level, but which puts its stamp on all life-expressions of that time, the Peasants' Wars, the Defenestration at Prague Castle, and finally the Thirty Years' War.

The demise of medieval magic was initiated by the Reformation and the rising humanism that naturally followed. Since the reformers traced back to early Jewish Christianity, which was based on the prophets but not on the orthodox magically-oriented Yahweh-cult, they therefore primarily fought against the magic foundation of Catholicism.

Catholicism, which was alien to Europe, meant a kind of flooding, and one is almost tempted to say - a "taking by surprise" - of the actual European developmental trends which emerged again at the time of humanism after having been suppressed for centuries. The collapse of Catholicism split the whole foundation on which magic in Europe had previously grown. Solely in France, which stayed Catholic, did some parts of magic remain, until the modern "spiritualism" was imported from America during the 19th century. Its mother soil was not impulsive demonism, but sentimental Puritanism.

As noteworthy as the scientific handling of occult sub-problems is today, most of what calls itself an "occult" or "theosophical" world view is flimsy and immature at best - the babbling of a late, senile time.

But to this day, every dwindling end has always been followed by a vigorous new beginning.

Dedication from Dr. Ernst Schertel to Adolf Hitler:

"Adolf Hitler – with venerated dedication from the author."

THEORY

While we present in the following a theory of magic, nothing will be further from our mind than to simply explain the phenomena away and portray everything as completely "natural." On the contrary, we want to show that the whole "addiction to naturalness" is a serious misunderstanding of "nature," that at the bottom of "nature" something tremendously "unnatural" is sleeping, and that every intellectual understanding only leads to the insight that the essence of things is beyond all intellect. That doesn't mean we should give up when we face problems when "our human insight is out of its depth," but it signifies an **advance of the intellect up to a point where it neutralizes itself, and it also signifies the apparently paradoxical fact of rationally explaining an irrational world aspect.**

European rationalism from the beginning should have gone another way, if the rationalism would have been consequential, but it always only went so far as the "common," that is to say the "average" sense permitted. Even the flight-attempts by Kant, which were carried out with a tremendous apparatus, landed, after some transcendental parades, in the harbour of Philistinism. Then came the nineteenth century with its so called "natural science," but which was never, except for the recent past, radical enough to surpass itself. As a pseudoscientific monstrosity its underlying world view dominated the masses, to then make way for a mediocre popular-occultism based on a liberal-Protestant foundation from which we still suffer today. But during the last several decades a truly scientific spirit ascended above these depths, opposing the roots of the pseudoscientific world view, and it has advanced so far that the problem of its own neutralisation is becoming acute. But at that moment when science distorts itself, the way will be clear for an above-scientific, that is to say, a magical world view.

The new scientific spirit manifested itself in various scientific disciplines: In the science of history as "cultural analysis," in medicine as "psychophysiology" and "psychoanalysis," and in the mathematical natural sciences as "theoretical physics and chemistry."

Cultural analysis as practiced by Nietzsche, Woringer, Spengler, Keyserling, Pannwitz, and others taught us the understanding of our own and of foreign cultures in their respective frameworks, and gave us, in contrast to the older science of history, truly above-European benchmarks for questions pertaining to different world views, but at the same time fostered deep scepticism towards our whole civilization. The psychophysiology of Schleich and others and the psychoanalysis of Freud initiated a whole new understanding of psychic phenomena and created insights into the essence of soul-body processes which the conventional orthodox psychology and anthropology would never have been able to give.

But the theoretical physics and chemistry with the "energetics" and "new-mechanistics" of Oswald, Mach, Goldschied, Auerbach, Zehnder, Mongrè, and many others set a complete overthrow of the pseudoscientific world view (that is partially still advocated by these thinkers) in motion, which is not yet fully understood by the "scientifically interested crowd," but is at least suspected with regard to catastrophes as represented by Einstein's theory of relativity.

For a theory of magic the results of the neo-mechanistic come primarily into question, since they principally touch the foundations of our "objective" world. From here on we will easily find the way to the psycho-physiologic and cultural analytic achievements.

The pseudoscientific oriented European believes himself to be surrounded by "things," which he regards as "objective," self-contained, static quantities. His "sensory organs" transmit to him the "perception" of these things, and for him it is only a question of looking accurately enough, to form a "correct" view about them and to not fall for an "appearance," a "deception." He thereby believes that an accurate view is indeed "equivalent" to the actual "things" of the environment.

This perception was soon weakened by the realisation that "things" are only accessible to us in accordance with our "sensory organs," that we would "observe" the things differently, poorer or richer, if we had other, more numerous or more limited sensory organs. How could there still be an "equivalent" between our mental image and the thing itself?! What we observed has always been only fragments. One did console oneself with the fact that fragments are still better than nothing and also that photography, for example, which describes things without colour and plastic etc., still conveys a sufficiently "true" view of things.

The matter didn't become problematic until one figured out the sham process which is the "depiction" of things on the part of our sensory organs. The comparison with the photographic camera was misleading for a long time. One did not take into consideration that the "thing," which we are seeing, and the "photography," which we are producing about it (the thing), are again only accessible to us through the "process of observation," and that therefore the well established relation between "thing" and "photography" did not apply to the process of observation, which remained as the big unknown quantity in an otherwise plausible equation. It was not possible to define the process of observation without again inserting it as an undefined quantity into the definition.

This whole perception became totally baseless ever since modern energetics began to dissolve the thing-concept itself. Kant retracted himself into the reservation of the "thing in itself" and provisionally agglutinated from there the world view of "common sense." Now, this was not possible anymore. If there were no "things" anyway there could be no "things in themselves," and then our "observations" could not be "depictions" of the things. The whole process of observation had to be explained in another way and our perception of the "thing-world" had to be considered on a new basis. But as soon as this happens the whole pseudoscientific world view, which we call "European" today, collapses in on itself.

Already during antiquity the view was held that things are not homogeneous complexes as we conceive them to be, but that they are formed by the assembling of infinitely small particles, which then, depending on their structure and connection, generate the characteristic attributes of the pertaining "thing." These smallest particles were called "atoms," because they were imagined as being indivisible. This atomic theory was adopted by modern physics and chemistry.

But the actual merits of the energetics were that it did not stop with this perception of the structure of things but that it further examined the atoms and the possible cohesive forces themselves. Hereby it came to light the atoms also were again not something homogeneous, but that they could be dissolved into systems of concentric assembled parts, which were, in the manner of the planets, circling around a central nucleus. Consequently things neither appeared as something homogenous nor as something static, but they instead appeared as being formed out of the smallest parts which were in whirring, circling motion. From there it was only a small step until the moment where one generally abandoned the "smallest parts," which were evermore splitting, and directed the attention more and more to the energetic side, to the "whirling forces" themselves. Therewith the last "solidness" of things was eliminated and the world was dissolved into a tension-net of forces. But even if one wanted to hold on to the "smallest parts," the basic fact was not affected: that "things" are nothing more than clouds of whirling tiny dusts which have retained nothing of the "thing-ness." But if we nonetheless observe "things," the process of observation cannot consist in a "process of depiction."

So, how do we gain our "observations," how do we gain our impression of "things"? The understanding is made much easier if one, instead of a "process of depiction," assumes an "interdependency" (correlation of effects) which is initially of an undetermined kind. Certain force-impulses "effectuate" at the level of our consciousness the emergence of certain "mental images," which we call "observations" but which have less "similarity" with the pertaining force as the bell-ringing with the electricity which is running it, or as a burn wound with the fire. Since at least two interacting powers belong to interdependency it is clear that our observation-images are not only caused by the force-lines of the "environment," but also by "us" ourselves, since we are after all **hit by the force-impulses. One describes this fact as the "subjective component" in the process of observation. Today it is still widely believed that the "being" of things is captured so much "more correctly" the more the subjective component is suppressed. But we see clearly that this component represents a necessary factor in the occurrence of observation-images and is no more excludable as the piston in a steam engine.**

Who actually is "we" with respect to our "environment"? The answer can only be found in the apparent paradox: we are a "part" of our "environment." We are indeed used to isolating our "I" as a closed whole from the rest of the cosmos and to sharply differentiate between our "I-world" (the microcosm) and the "environment" (the macrocosm). But on second thought we actually do not exactly know where our "I" begins and where it ends. The borderline for most humans is probably at the skin surface of their body, since that is as far as their immediate sphere of feeling is ranging. This specification is nonetheless entirely arbitrary. Some humans are able to expand their sphere of feeling beyond their skin surface; others have such a rudimentary feeling of their body that they hardly feel their extremities belong to them. And still for others nothing "bodily" belongs to their actual "I," it is rather thought of as "purely mental," even so far that certain sensual-spiritual emotions are felt as "alien to I."

Our "I" in the strict sense of the word is nothing else but a "focal point," a "center of consciousness," a "knot" within the infinite cosmic force-net, in itself completely meaningless and only the principle of the dawning of consciousness. But what we call "I" in the sense of concrete personality, real individuality, etc. is already a complex of "elements of observation," and principally does not differ from the tangible "environment." Our "body," our "soul" etc. are fundamentally nothing but certain complexes of observation like a tree, a house, a star, or another "thing."

That we nevertheless compare our own person to the environment and often frantically defend it is due to the fact that our capability of consciousness is only connected with the cosmic force-net at that point, which we call our "I," and therefore this point possesses outstanding importance for us. Therefore our "body," as the first surrounding layer of the "environment," is equipped with infinitely more rich and sensitive cords of perception than those which connect the more distant layers of the universe with the "I-center." Whole solar systems can perish and perhaps we hardly notice anything about it, while the tiniest dust particle which penetrates into our eye, the tiniest blood vessel which bursts in our brain, leads to the most intense sensations. Our body is the stronghold of our consciousness, and our "I-center" is the point where the world forces converge for us and gain meaning.

Our body represents an accumulation of potential and kinetic world energies and ranges on the way from the line of our ancestors, to animal, plant, and crystal down to the

beginning of all things. In our body rests like sediment the whole past of the world, beginning with the first stardust. Through our bodies flood the energies of the universe, out of the infinite into the infinite. They propel the mill of our being. What we call our "soul" is the sum of all world energies, all pasts of the world and states of the world, which we darkly-emotionally realize. This is the secret of the "inside view." When the mystic closes his eyes and devotes himself only to the emotional perceptions of his "inner self," that is to say devotes himself to a certain layer of his "body," then he is experiencing the whole infiniteness of the cosmic which is resting in this "body." But as soon as he opens his eyes, again he is confronted with a chaotic disorder of "things" with which he does not really know how to deal with. The combined view, the synopsis of world forces is easier by means of the "inside view" than the "outside view." The old peoples nevertheless also possessed the deepness of the "outward view," and on this double-visibility rested their culture, their creative power, and last but not least their magic.

That we, who are living today, do not really know how to deal with the "sensory world," that it appears to be empty, dull, even oftentimes annoying, that we perceive our body as a "prison" of our "soul," that we are consequently at best able for mystique, and only in the rarest cases capable of magic, is because of the extinguishing of the ability which all late times are lacking, and which consists in experiencing the "outer world" as an incarnation of "spiritual" contents. But only he is a magician who is able to inspire things and solidify the soul.

The difference between "soul" or "inner world" and sensual "environment" or "outer world" consists only in that the "soul" represents a complex of "emotional perceptions," the "outer world" a complex of "sensory perceptions," of "pictures." It is not possible to draw an exact border between both areas, since spiritual-emotional moments easily gain a pictorial nature, and on the other side every sensory perception carries a more or less pronounced "emotional tone" provided that it not only consists of an "emotion," as is the case with the senses of smell and taste and with various kinds of irritations of the skin.

On the fact that emotional moments fade into pictorial perceptions, and on the other side pictorial sensory impressions are associated with more or less strong emotional complexes, rests the whole phenomenon of the "inspiriting of nature," which represents the basis of animism and demonism and thereby of all magical aspects.

The magician has to possess the ability to transform "emotions" into "things" and to capture "things" emotionally. We explain this aspect psychologically with a so-called "capability of projection" on the one side and a strong "ability to empathize" on the other side. Both are basically the same, and are the result of strong inner-body vigour and intense correlation between the various layers of the body-sphere. These qualities are more or less extinguished with regards to the average modern European, but they existed in primitive man and can still be found in that type which we call "hysterical."

A certain degree of hysteria was always part of the magical man, but this type who was in such a way "burdened" or "gifted" was not always so set apart from his folk-comrades as is the case today. Primitive mankind in its entirety was to a much larger degree "hysterical" than today's mankind. What hysteria actually is was first accurately defined by C.L. Schleich: "Hysteria itself is not a disease of the nervous system, it is also not a mostly paroxysmal autointoxication of the organism, generated by inner secretion of the body-glands, but it is a perversion of the fantasy-activity. Its being rests upon an abnormal penetration of the fantasy-streams of the right cerebral hemisphere into the activity of the body tissue, which signifies an abnormality. Usually to a lesser extent (with regards to a completely healthy human) the imagination reaches only the fabric of the body-forms of the periphery. The hysteria contains a metaphysical secret which still needs to be unravelled, more peculiar and more miraculous than any spiritualistic occurrence, more intriguing than all appearances of occult procedures which have been studied until now, also more astonishing than all claimed or proven Fakir-exhibitions of the Indians; it is a real seat of magic and a temple of the Mayas, which willingly operates with appearances of ghosts, formations of horror, spectres, and Fata Morgana mirages. Hysteria is a special case of the creation out of an idea... and I want to touch upon this subject, because here we can discover the most illustrious examples of the transition of the subjective idea into objective truth."

Here it is distinctly pronounced what we mean: the close correlation of the "spiritual" with the "material" and the fact of a direct transition of "emotions" into material-perceivable "realities" of the so called "outer world." But this is the foundation of all magic.

We have described our I-center, our center of consciousness, as a point within the cosmic force-net.

This point represents a place of crossing, a whirl-center of cosmic force-lines and is connected with the whole cosmos like a knot in a fishnet with the net itself. We have defined our "soul" and in addition our "body" as layers of the force-net, which are lying around that knot and are (as surrounding meshes) particularly close and directly (because of the "inner-feeling" or "organ-feeling") intertwined with it. The layers of the cosmic dynamic which are further away are only indirectly accessible by use of the body-sphere.

There was until now no talk of "things" in the general sense, since forces are not things, but are the above-material ("para-cosmical") roots of consciousness-phenomena, which in some circumstances gain "thing character." How do we now arrive at the so-called "observation" of "things," which in the energetic sense do not even exist?

We have to imagine our body as a seismograph of the cosmic dynamic. Shifting of energy within the cosmic force-net "effectuate," by indirect way via our body, a "perception" on the table of our consciousness, just as any shaking of the earth causes, by indirect way via the seismograph, a curve on a strip of paper. This curve is the result of joint action of the shaking of the earth together with the individual parts of the seismograph. If, for example, there is red ink in its pen, then the curve will be red, if there is black ink in it, then the curve will be black. Depending on the construction of the machine, the curve will be high and narrow or low and wide, even though the shaking of the earth was neither red nor black, nor narrow or wide.

The same applies to our "observations." They are the result of the co-action between cosmic shifting of energy and the force-complex of our body. But they are as little equal to the shifting of energy as an earthquake is to a red or black curve.

It is in the nature of every perception and consequently of every observation that it is standing before us, that is to say "projected." Our consciousness automatically puts the mental image "before us" and creates therewith an "outer world" or "environment." So, perceptions are always something which originated in the co-action between the cosmic and our own inner-bodily energies, but are never the copy-image of a "thing." Things only exist at our level of consciousness, and they are drawn upon this level by the whole universe on its way through our body, which itself is just a part of the universe.

There exists no consciousness without body, just as no earthquake-curve can exist without a seismograph. Every center of consciousness creates a specific individual environment or thing-world, just as every seismograph draws its own curve. We only believe that there exists just one "objective thing-world." But cultural analysis gave us the proof that different peoples envision totally different "worlds," which are in themselves completely reasonable but are nonetheless inconsistent with one another. The idea of a "multitude of worlds" thereby gains total confirmation. Paul Mongré spoke about this: "There need not be only the one continuum of world conditions, wherein we are interwoven; in addition to this there are any number of other worlds thinkable, with variable content, displayed on timelines, on which points of presence play their game. That means a pluralité des mondes, which we have to accept, especially because we are not able to assure ourselves of it by experience, but are always depending on our one timeline."

Now the objection is suggested that in this way every differentiation between "fantastical perceptions" ("imaginations") and "objective observations" might be blurred. But there is indeed no fundamental difference between them. Imagination and observation are to the same extent products of the cosmic dynamic and of inner-bodily forces and as such are "real," provided that the notion of "reality" still has any meaning at all. That in practice we nevertheless differentiate between imagination and observation is because of the fact that the imagination is to a stronger degree caused by inner-bodily compression of cosmic energy, observation on the other hand is caused more by the influence of layers of the cosmic force-net which are further "away." These distinguishing features can be very important for daily life, but they do not play any role in relation to "true" or "false," "real" or "illusory." The notions of "true" and "false" are completely relative and depend on the overall meaning of our world of perception, just as the meaning of an individual word always depends on the overall meaning of the whole sentence, or even the whole book.

None of our perceptions, whether "imagination" or "observation," can be related to any "thing," since facts of consciousness do not originate in "things," but are the stuff of possible "things." So, no perception can per se be described as "true" or "wrong," as "right" or "false," as "real" or "illusory," since all these notions always require an existing thing-world beyond our perception. If a perception is "true" or "wrong" is ultimately only a question of intensity. There are perceptions which reach as far as the material (thing) intensity and others which get stuck in a faint, illusive quality. Here we also have to quote C.L. Schleich: "Everything spiritual - if wrong, if right - if infected, like the bacilli, quickly overreaches the rhythm of the **thought: thus thoughts have gained their great power over the masses. Ideas are infectious, and irrefutable tensions of consideration extracted from the fantasy of the individual, concentrations of the mind into explosive, dynamite-like structures turn into that agglomerated flake, which originated from the step of a bird in the snow and finally becomes an avalanche."**

Those perceptions which find the best breeding ground within a given world of consciousness and unfold the highest intensity prevail and are then believed to be "true." Even the enlightened European of today is living from imaginations in the amount of three quarters. The great cultures of the past are in general not thinkable without imaginative ideas.

Our "body" represents, as we already indicated, a certain quantum of "potential" or "latent" cosmic energy. Over the course of time it built itself up by the absorption ("assimilation") of cosmic forces and it continually takes more quanta of energy in by eating, breathing, radiations of heat and light, magnetic influence, sound, pressure, etc. We call this process "energetic re-absorption." Our body likewise constantly emits energy into the rest of the cosmos in the form of muscle work, nervous activity, breathing, thermo-magnetic radiation and all kinds of excretions. During this process the latent quantities of energy transform again into "actual" or "kinetic" energy. A part of the forces, roused from their latency, is instantly again bound in the body itself, that is to say lead back into the potential form. We call this "energy accumulation."

The aforementioned processes together result in the "energetic cycle." Our body is therefore integrated into the electric circuit of the universe, just like an electric motor in a machine.

Our world of perception, that is to say our "world" as such, has a much entangled foundation. What we call our "body" is itself only a "perception," which is created at our level of consciousness by certain complexes of energy. To be precise, we would always need to discriminate between our energetic body-sphere and our material perception-body.

The thing-world dissolved completely over the course of our contemplation and changed into a pure structure of perception. We almost arrived at the standpoint of the "solipsistic idealism." The only remaining reality is the one that lies in the cosmic dynamic, which is for us completely unsubstantial and bodiless, and lies in the "energetic para-cosmos," which has nothing to do with our imagined universe other than that it somehow gives rise to the emergence of this **perception. The difference between "true" and "false" has disappeared. We have only gained one thing: An insight into the structure, that is to say into the "drawing floor" of that jugglery of fantasy, which we call the "objective world." But quite a lot is gained with it: namely the possibility to intervene in this structure, that is to say change the world according to our will. But this is magic, and on this basis we are able to create reality where no reality is.**

God was also alone in his bodiless, being-less eternity and created the world out of nothing. If we saturate ourselves with the godly, demonic, para-cosmic forces, if we increase our dream-force until it bears "things," then we can also create worlds.

To clarify this issue we have to go into further detail about the essence of the imagination. Imaginations emerge when latent energies of the body-sphere are released, either by any inner-bodily process or as a result of a perhaps unconscious process of absorption. This impact of energy then spreads to more extensive and deeper lying force-focuses and arouses in this manner enormous energy quanta from their latency, **sums of energy, which perhaps were already absorbed by our ancestors from the cosmos and grew stronger over the course of centuries and millenniums. Darker memories are appearing, at first maybe only emotionally, but gradually taking a more and more definite material form. In this way, the emerged imagination is now projected to the outside and appears there as "hallucination" or as "reality," depending on whether it can be brought into accordance with our other world of consciousness or not.**

What we call "objective observation" is only a special case of the imagination. An "observation" emerges in an, as immediate as possible, connection with an absorbed complex of energy (a "sensory impression"), but since primeval times the body has accumulated energies, having the most to do with regards to the imagination in the wider sense. But the "becoming-an-image of the cosmic dynamic" is both, and only that is what counts for us here.

As soon as those big complexes of accumulated energy break through during the process of the imagination, a process of emission of the strangest kind becomes noticeable: this energy begins at first to change the structure of the body-sphere and if sufficient energy is present spreads furthermore into the connection of forces of the rest of the cosmos. The change of the body-structure manifests in the manner that the body tries to bring itself into accordance with the content of the imagination. This phenomenon can grow so much that new shapes are directly appearing inside of the body-sphere, that individual tissues or whole organs increase or decrease in volume, their functions grow, cease or change, that dramatic metamorphoses happen inside the nerve centers, in the composition of the blood, and finally in the whole habit of the pertaining personality, which bring about a totally new attitude towards existence and the triggering of unknown abilities.

C.L. Schleich explained explicitly, "that the function-play of the fantasy, that is to say the sum of the functions of all which constitutes the notion of the capability of perception, exerts a visual, shaping, plastic influence on the physical happenings in the body and on the operation of the cell-mechanisms" and "that the fantasy is able to gain entrance in every body tissue through the fences and enclosures of the cell-structures and of the mechanisms of the blood circuit as well as of the peripheral nerve streams."

This formative power of the imagination is not only limited to the pertaining body, but once initiated the process of emission of energy can also spread beyond the body surface to the other surrounding cosmic layers, which then possibly subject to its influence. That the imagination is able to gain power over the objects of the environment is fundamentally no more mysterious than the fact that a simple figment of the imagination is enough to cause nausea in us, and "telekinesis" is no stranger than the fact that we are able to move our extremities with a simple act of volition.

In contrast to the "empirical" effect on things, which becomes possible because of our muscles and tools, we refer to the effectiveness of the imagination as "magical." The border between both forms is overlapping, since the empirical effects also have a certain imaginative foundation.

Today's man resists these insights. He raves about "empiricism" and rejects all "imaginations." He does not know that his empirical world view, in which he takes great pride, also ultimately rests on imaginations. Every world view is built on an imaginative basic-synthesis. Even the most palpable "facts" only exist if we do not discuss certain basic ideas, which are quite imaginative, but believingly accept them.

Here it is the same as with the constellations. These are constructed from individual observations of stars, which we combine with imaginary lines to certain figures. But the individual observations of the stars are also on a sticky wicket, since some of these stars do not exist any more, and they are all not standing at the places any more where we are "observing" them, as a result of the deflection of the ray of light.

After these contemplations it won't seem totally unjustified if we assign the primacy within our living activities to the imagination, particularly given that without it not only a "world view" would be impossible, but that we would also get to no "doing" or "acting" whatsoever, since all our aims, evaluations, and ideals are exclusively imaginative in origin.

The man with the greatest force of imagination is commanding of the world and creates realities according to his will, instead of being the slave of an unsubstantial, bodiless empiricism. Empiricism fulfils the laws of "probability," but imagination makes the impossible happen. The pure empirical man is the entropic type, which leads to the complete devaluation of cosmic energy, the imaginative man instead, the magician, is the actual focus of the ektropic, the renewal of the world, remodelling of the world, the new birth of being. Felix Auerbach, the creator of the physical theory of life, articulated these facts in the following way: "Everything in the world, as far as it is of an active character, always aspires to the more probable state; it is anxious, so to speak, to fulfil the laws of the statistic. But it is obviously the signature of everything individual, everything specifically ektropic, that it accomplishes the improbable, that it knocks the statistic on its head. The truly ektropic is always new, improbable, perplexing, a scoff at the statistic, or, if it is spreading and prevailing, founding a new statistic, because the most improbable can become probable by the power of its influence."

As a result of our physical-epistemic analyses, we have now arrived at the definition of magic: Magic is autogenic exertion of power on the basis of imagination. And we have gained a new definition for the notion of reality. Reality is the becoming-an-image of our deepest essential powers. "Truth" is nothing receptive, but something creative, the "process of observation," not a process of "depiction" but of "construction."

The man who lets his powers of imagination grow until the creation of material reality is a magician. He possesses that primeval double-visibility, which not only enables him to perform the inside view, but also opens to him a world of pictures, things, and forms, which he creates himself and pulsates them with the forces of the universe.

Thus he differs from the mere "mystic," who flees every created reality and never lets his inner-body energies come up to the point of becoming-an-image. As a result of this flight before the concreteness, the pure mystic is not able to unfold magic effects, but must always be content with mere emotional immersion into the non-pictorial dynamic of the cosmic.

We call the central focus of the cosmic forces in us our "god" or our "demon." It describes the punctual projection of the whole dynamic of the universe with all of its abysmal infiniteness in our self, it signifies the deepest sense, the first being and the highest value, created in the center of our consciousness out of the senseless, being-less and value-less chaos of paracosmic forces. This parthenogenesis of the god in us, this primeval creation of a sense out of the senseless, is the darkest secret of existence, and is the actual "principium individuationis," the actual "act of creation" and withstands every thinking dissection and every potential imagination that it itself might be the origin and foundation of every thought and every imagination.

Due to the fact that it is concentrated in one point, the god-center itself is without image or matter and coincides with "nothingness." Consequently, it also stops being an "event," a "phenomenon of consciousness," because a consciousness, an event without matter, an imagination without something imagined, is a contradiction in terms. Here it is not different than with other things. They also possess reality only as part of their phenomenality and dissolve completely as soon as one wants to erase this phenomenality. The god-center also possesses reality only as far as it assumes any kind of phenomenality, be it a gloomy or a glaring "feeling," be it a more or less clear cut "plastic" in the proper sense of the word "pictorial" sensation. Just as the cosmic forces in their linear fragmentation dissolve the perception of "things" and of "objects" in us, so do these forces in their point-concentration create a corresponding "perception," which is the most significant, the most saturated with sense, the most intrinsically valued of all perceptions, the concrete perception of god. This perception is just as little "right" or "false" as any other material sensation, because perceptions are autogenic, self-being essentialities, which do not "resemble" or "not resemble" other essentialities apart from their own, but which possess their reality in their "phenomenality." They are arguably "created" by para-cosmic realities, but they cannot be equated with them just as a curve with an earthquake or as a symptom of poisoning with the poison. So it is foolish to ask if our perception of a deity is "right," just as this question has turned out to be foolish with regards to other things. The act of perception itself is always the act of creation of the imagined matter.

It is therefore also senseless to claim that the deity might be "without image," since it is emerging from the point-concentration of non-pictorial, para-cosmic forces. The pictorial nature or non-pictorial nature of the perception of god depends only on our power.

The magical man is now, as we have already indicated, a man with the highest abilities, with such a great creative "power of projection" that he is able to affect every perception until it reaches the last material reality. His perception of god will therefore be pictorial. The mystic, on the other hand, is a man who has indeed a deep capacity for experience, but little power. His perception of god is therefore non-pictorial, that is to say it gets stuck at a preliminary stage to becoming-an-image, at the line of the mere "emotional."

The magician is not content with experiencing his "god" merely emotionally, but with the imagination he lets him take shape and integrates him materially into the environment. For this purpose he projects his perception of god into the surrounding space and localizes it at a certain place. This process can happen voluntarily or involuntarily, but it involves in any case that which is called "theophany," that is to say the becoming-an-image of the god on a hallucinatory basis. Such theophany is very rare and requires a special power of the imagination-sphere. More frequent are vaguer face- or acoustic-hallucinations and phenomena of compression, which are by themselves already highly advanced, but are also only preliminary stages to completely becoming-an-image.

Since the mere hallucinatory basis is only in the rarest cases enough to achieve the intended compression of the god-perception, another psychic process is brought into it, which then safely guarantees the embodiment of the god. This is the process which is psychiatrically called "the process of illusion." Here, an autogenic perception is not freely transferred into space, but the psyche grasps a perceived object of the empirical environment and projects the imaginative perception on it. This perception connects itself closely with the pertaining object, so that this object is conceived as the realisation of the perception. The process of illusion manifests itself in an imaginative transmutation of the "meaning-value," of the "sense" or the "metaphysical substance" of an empirical object, but its physical substance remains completely unchanged. This process is therefore called "trans-substantiation" in the hieratic language, while only reflecting on the metaphysical substance, on the imaginative "meaning-value" of the object. In this manner the imaginatively loaded object is called an "idol," a "fetish" or psychologically speaking an "imago-spurious," that is to say an imaginative bastard-creation.

The realisation of god-perception rests upon an utterly individual act. The creation of the empirical environment is indeed also such a pure individual act, but nevertheless a great number of various individuals can participate in one and the same empirical environment (practically speaking), since the process of observation, by which the empirical environment is emerging, is not touching the actual deep structure of the individuality. This is different with regards to god-perception. It originates in the deepest center of the self and is therefore to a high degree exclusively individual, so that it does not have meaning for other individual. We call perceptions which originate in these deep structures "demonic perceptions," and we call the environment which is created by them "demonic environment" or "world of demons." Demons are therefore not "empirical" essentialities, we are not able to simply become aware of them with "observation," but they are to a high degree of purely imaginative origin and emerge from cosmic energies which are compressed in the body. They are nonetheless "real" in the proper phenomenal sense just like empirical objects.

That nevertheless certain demonic perceptions often have meaning for large groups of individuals can be ascribed to the fact that every kind of "perception" is infectious, especially if a similar structure is present in the deep structures of the pertaining individuals.

It would be senseless to set the demonic perceptions as "fictional" against the empirical observations, since ultimately the empirical world is also "fictional," rests on an imaginative basic-synthesis, that is to say the empirical "reality" is in its root of "demonic" or – which is the same – "magical" nature.

All magic is demonism, since both notions signify in the same way the principle of the imagination. That nonetheless magical effects spring from certain people, without us being able to demonstrate a conscious world of perception at them has nothing to do with it, since there also exist unconscious magical-demonic effects, as can be determined with regards to stones, plants, etc. But the consciously working magician will always feel himself surrounded by a more or less clearly structured demonic world.

Every demonic-magical world is centered towards the great individuals, from whom basic creative conceptions spring. Every magician is surrounded by a force field of para-cosmic energies, and as already indicated he acts to the highest degree "ektropically" upon the cosmic dynamic. The individuals which are infected by him form a "community" or his "people" (Volk) and create a complex of life of a certain

imaginative framework which is called "culture." From that moment on, when these imaginative-magical forces of cohesion run dry, the result is a deteriorating people (Volk) and with them, their culture. Felix Auerbach expressed this as following: "The cosmos takes direct interest only in strong and ektropic individuals. Consequently it follows that the cosmos takes no substantial interest in the number, in a - as high as possible - number of individuals. This particular ektropical influence never springs from the masses but always only from the few, who, by increasing the selective foresight to the highest degree, are ahead of their time.

Since the magical world always represents something concretely directional and individually centered, it is clear that every kind of tendency of abstraction or universalism is destructive to it. Tendencies of abstraction and universalism are symptoms of the old age of a culture, and since the "aging" is starting relatively early, from a physiologic-energetic point of view, the already mentioned fact is explained that historically we only know magical worlds heading south, that is to say that the history of magic essentially appears to us as a "history of decline." This fact was also formulated by Felix Auerbach theoretically-physically: "The ektropic effecting ability sets in at the beginning, increases up to a maximum, then soon afterwards sinks and goes away. In most cases the beginning takes place right away with a finite value.., the ascent to the maximum is generally very steep, so therefore the aging sets in very early. There are even cases where the optimum almost coincides with the beginning."

In consequence of the energetic origin of the god-perception and of the demonic in general, it participates in the two basic-characteristics or potentialities-of-existence of everything energetic, namely in motion and rest or in actuality and potentiality, or in the Auerbach-sense in ektropism and entropism. This double-sidedness of the energetic manifests itself in the demonic reality in terms of the polarity of the "satanic" and "seraphic." The satanic means kinetic, actuality, ektropism or "free energetic valence," the seraphic on the other hand is latency, potentiality, entropism or "bound energetic valence." Since all actuality drifts towards potentiality, so also does the satanic strive towards the seraphic. As soon as the state of latency, the entropy is reached, somewhere a new center of kinetic energy has to break open, in order that with its ektropic effectiveness the final entropization of the whole cosmos is again postponed for a while.

"Satan" is the creative, value-setting and value-increasing principle, which at first always appears "evil," "Seraph" on the other hand is the resting, preserving, values- effecting pole, which we call "good." Satan is the fertilizing, destroying/constructing warrior; Seraph is possession and peace. Satan and Seraph are therefore not "opposites," which one could tear apart, but they are "pole-notions," which are only thinkable in each other and with each other.

The demonic is like everything energetic and therefore in its root "satanic," but drifts over the course of its activity towards the construction of a "seraphic," self-contained, and resting world. The separation of "white" from "black" magic" is therefore nonsense, and mere pretense. Because here "white" means only as much as "permitted," and "black" means "forbidden." But this is completely relative and depends only on the presently dominant and hence "justified" and "right" recognized basic-synthesis. This distinction becomes even more unsubstantial if it is applied to the social-moral area and "black" magic is defined as the "egoistic" and "white" as "social" or "altruistic." Because it is not currently acceptable to debate why the advantages of an arbitrary "multiplicity" should be valued higher morally than the advantage of individuals. Nietzsche already debated this sufficiently and Felix Auerbach also screened this problem from an energetic point of view: "Concerning ethics, the juxtaposition: egoism and altruism are banal and not crucial **for the main point. Only the antithesis is crucial: ektropism and entropism. Egoism can be good, and altruism can be bad. Service makes great, but dominance makes greater. What is allowed** depends not only on the What but also on the Who. Allowed is finally what pleases the cosmos; even more than allowed: wished-for. The ektropic efficiency and net-effect of an ingenious lifestyle and life work would be lowered more by common mob-ethics than the cosmic police would likely allow. Quod non licet bovi, tamen licet Jovi."

The only "law" the magician is subordinated to is the will of his "god" or "demons," that is to say the ektropic effect resulting from the cosmic forces which are compressed in him. So the magician is always "black" and "white" in one, just like the passage of the Kabbalah presented god, as was already cited in the historical part. Around this one basic law are layered several regulations and rules to which the magician subjects himself to, in order to organise more intimate communion with the demon and saturate himself with ever-new para-cosmic forces. But whether he wants to put the - in this way - gained power into the commission of a multiplicity or use it for his own ends, **is completely left to his discretion. The "people" (Volk) he might gather around himself have nothing to do with an abstract multiplicity, whose "good" he would have to "serve," but represent an enlargement of his I-sphere. But it already has happened that a magician abandoned, shattered, or castigated his own people, if** they did not seem reactive enough anymore. Christ is the historical example for this, who originally came to the Jews, but then went to the heathens. Also Moses, as incarnated Yahweh, often castigated his people as he was uplifting them.

The "people" (Volk) of the magician are always opposed to abstract "humanity" and random "multiplicity," and at first are therefore conceived just as "evil" as the magician himself. Not until the magical world is consolidated and has prevailed will the satanic root be "latent," that is to say impalpable, and everything which happens in accordance with this world is also now appearing - even to the most harmless mind - as "good," just as the most intense movement appears as standing still if the whole environment is moving in the same direction.

But some day every magical people, that is to say every "culture," falls prey to the opposing forces, even if these should have spared the magician himself. This end appears as the ghost of the "Anti-Christ," of whom all magical people knew and whose entrance into his world he would like to postpone as long as possible (until the "end of times").

The magician is the heroic man, who, despite being conscious of his tragic life-line, is still following it – for the will of the demon who is pushing him. The magician is the climax of mankind, is a nucleus of the highest ektropic force and therefore appears as an embodiment of the last cosmic meaning, an ambassador of the deity.

The cosmic forces, in realising their becoming-an-image, always depend on a particular I-center, conversely every I-center would be ineffective if it would not be pulsated with cosmic energies. Hereupon rests the interaction and mutual conditionality of "demon" and "magician" or of "god" and "human." Without the magician the demonic forces would have never reached embodiment, and without the demon the magician would be bare of any kind of deep forces. This fact was still well known to the late mystics of the middle ages and Angelus Silesius wrote a much-cited verse about it.

Out of the mutual conditionality of demon and magician grows the necessity of association between them, which can increase from the simplest emotional immersion up to bloody bodily unification, depending on the intensity and image-power of the acting energies.

Between demon and magician, that is to say between the para-cosmic forces and the pertaining empirical body wherein these are acting, exists a continuous polar tension, which on the one hand manifests itself in the creation of an enormous "distance," by making the image of the demon as enormous, as big, as distant and unfamiliar as possible, and on the other hand by arranging the amalgamation with this image (the "communion") as immense, and complete. The bodily communion or the "sacrifice" is carried out in a way that the magician is either inducing the appearance of the demon on a hallucinatory basis and thereby unifying himself with him or that he is using an imago-spurious, that is to say an object of the empirical environment, upon which the demonic force-complex is projected. Both forms are historically attested. J.W. Hauer writes about this: "We know unambiguously from various sources that the gods appeared to their worshippers and filled them with strength and enthusiasm, in order that the singer or thinker felt himself unified with the deity during the sacrifice. The excited singers report again and again that they had come and did their deeds in companionship and friendship with the sacrifice-makers, they lead the way and escorted them. It seems reasonable to assume that primitive Yoga was above all else a summoning of the gods."

This involves a becoming-an-image of the demon and communion on a hallucinatory basis. Carl Einstein expressed about the imago-spurious form of the communion: "The sculptor treats his work as a deity or as the deity's custodian: from the very outset, he maintains a distance from his work because this work either is or contains a specific god. The sculptor's labour is a form of remote adoration and the work is therefore something autonomous, more powerful than its maker; the more so as he infuses it with all his intensity and, as the weaker being, he sacrifices to it. His labour must be described as religious worship. The resulting piece, as a deity, is free and independent of everything else; both worker and worshiper are at an immeasurable distance from the work. The latter will never be involved in human events except as something powerful and again distanced. The transcendence of the work is both determined by and presumed in religiosity. It is created in adoration, in terror of god, and terror is also its effect. Maker and worshipper are merged psychologically, which is to say essentially identical;

the effect resides not in the work of art but in its pre-established, unquestioned being as a god. It is the god, who maintains his closed mythical reality, taking in the worshipper, transforming him into a mystical being, annulling his human existence." In the Catholic cult the imago-spurious form of the sacrifice and adoration is still purely preserved.

The sacrifice is necessary in the cosmic context, since the demons (the ektropic centers of energy) feed upon the sacrifice, that is to say only gain power over a world system by contact with a real body, and the magician adheres with the sacrifice those powers to him, that is to say he centers them on his person, amalgamates with them and subordinates them to his will. The demons demand the bodies and the magician demands the demonology, and both find fulfilment in the communion of the sacrifice.

The cosmic dynamic charge, which is created by demonic communion, molds the magician into a more comprehensive tool of the para-cosmic forces, so that finally nothing seems impossible to him. He is enabled to change his body sphere, enlarge, narrow, or completely relocate it and in this way transfer it into different kinds of energetic aggregate phases. But he is also able to exert magical - that is to say highly complex - energetic effects, beyond his body-sphere.

On the reallocation of the body sphere rest those phenomena which are generally associated with the so called "astral body." The astral body is nothing empirically substantial which is part of the "material" body, but this notion simply describes a certain condition of the whole body sphere, wherein it has a great instability of its molecular cohesion and is in an outstanding close connection with the cosmos. Upon this condition rests phenomena like clairvoyance, invisibility, permeation of solid objects, and much more. All these phenomena are explained by the fact that our body sphere is quite relative with regards to its boundary and is more or less labile in its constitution, this therefore means that the border of our feel- and action-sphere does not necessarily coincide with our skin surface, and that the complex we call our "body" is able, as a result of its energetic structure, to assume different physical forms, like water, for example, and not only in its fluid but also in its solid and gaseous states.

Clairvoyance and clairaudience rest upon the diffuse expansion of our feel-sphere, so that processes which are beyond our normal body-sphere come into our consciousness, just like inner-bodily processes. That we are at the same time also able to look at future events becomes understandable if we remember that an astronomer, as a result of the expansion of his observation- and sense-sphere (astronomical experience and astronomical tools), is also able to recognize upcoming events from the present constellation of the stars (solar eclipses, transits, collisions etc.) Therefore, clairvoyance does not mean "all-knowingness," as is sometimes claimed, but it has its borders and possibilities of error, just like empirical prognoses. It always depends on the capabilities of the practitioner and on certain energetic constellations of the cosmos.

Just like clairvoyance, the so-called "emission of the astral body" also requires an expansion of the feel-sphere ("expulsion of sensibility"), but in this case the sensibility is located to a certain distant place. In addition to this comes a charging of this space-point with energetic action ability, in order that not only impressions can be absorbed but also dynamic effects can be performed. This would be similar to constructing a station for wireless telegraphy at a distant place in connection with the installation of wireless detonation of mines, etc. The compression of inner-bodily energy at the distant place can become so great that persons who are present there can themselves have the vision of the man from whom the effect is springing, so that a "duplication" of his body seems to be the case.

"Levitation," "invisibility," and "permeation of solid objects" all theoretically represent no impossibility, but are explainable on the basis of our energetic approach. They only require such an enormous shifting of the body in its innermost structure (inversion of gravity, dissolution of the molecular cohesion etc.) that they should indeed be rare as an empirical phenomenon. In most cases it will be a matter of influence on the audience on a hallucinatory basis in connection with certain telekinetic and telepathic effects.

All these magic acts are initiated at first in fantasy with a distinct and concentrated perception of the goal that is to be achieved. The concentration of this perception is significantly supported by all possible empirical arrangements, creation of certain objects like signs, pictures, etc., certain postures and motions, and insertion of certain toxins into the body, in short all of that which can be called "magical manipulations". The various kinds of "dance-magic," with which we already have become acquainted, furthermore the "image- and amulet-magic," the "augural-magic," etc. are among them.

Concentration in connection with the magical measures leads to the auto-suggestive perception of the goal that is to be achieved, and this perception is now acting as the special ektropic nucleus upon the body sphere and beyond it into the whole cosmos.

Every special kind of magic therefore represents only a special case of the phenomenon, which leads to the becoming-an-image, that is to say the realisation of the demon which we have already described in detail.

The actual value of magic does not rest on the performing of special magical arts, that is to say on what is called "conjuring" in the popular sense of the word. Special magical abilities can often coincide with a very low overall standard of the pertaining person, just like completely inferior people often can possess a fabulous talent for mental arithmetic. As important and useful such capabilities are practically, only the one whose whole being is magically centered and therefore possesses the sacral basic tone which we perceive with regards to the great initiated ones should be called a magician in the high sense. To aglow the whole life in this manner is the meaning of magic and its intrinsic value. Magic in this great meaning has the characteristic to relate the person with the cosmic powers, and to connect him in this way with the roots and source of all existence. At its height magic coincides with religion. All great magicians have been great religious persons.

We have seen that magic stirs the darkest abysses of existence. That it has a satanic side like everything alive must not mislead us into condemning it, because this would be a condemnation of the cosmic powers themselves, which are weaving the Fata Morgana of existence. There have been world views which have rejected being for this reason, renounced it and negated it, for example the doctrine of Buddha or Schopenhauer. But this is religious negativism, which is negating the will of the gods and is pushing them back into nothingness. From this attitude springs a resigned pessimism, nihilism, and atheism, which can never act as culture-creating.

The being is purified by its meaning. But this meaning lies in the "mind," not in abstract, rational thinking and merely scientific observations, but only in the concrete formation and event, in the irrational, intuitional product of the cosmic dynamic. The essence of things is not captured by dissolution of their phenomenal connection. Compressions of cosmic forces, which are senseless in isolation, only bear meaning in connection with the intuition. Only with intuition are we able to dominate the cosmic dynamic as a whole and are thus capable of controlling it according to our will. Only in the intuition, in the image, steps the infiniteness of the cosmic in our I-circle and operates the deepest form of reality and power: the demon, the god.

Without gods and service to them existence sinks into an empty profanity and loses any kind of meaning.

Reproduction of the Hitler bookplate
found in his copy of *Magic*

PRACTICE

All magic emanates from the body and from the incarnated, from the pictorial-material appearance of existence (there-being). That the body and "things" only possess "phenomenal reality" has nothing to do with it, since there exists no other "reality" for any kind of consciousness than the one of "perception," the "object," and the "appearance". But in a reality without consciousness we would only have nonsense. The body and things are the basic contents of existence and "divinization of the body" and "embodiment of god" are the axis of all magic. What Friedrich Gundolf said about antique life in its entirety applies especially to magic and its emissions. "They are all only thinkable among people who are affirming the sensually limited existence, sanctify, divinize, and typify the invisible as force, instinct, felt as fate, anticipated notional life. Thereby one must not fashionably perceive the body as a physiological apparatus, but as a metaphysical essence, and not perceive divinization as a psychological experience, "deification," but as a cultic act and a mythical display... The cultic act of god-embodiment is the sanctification, the magic, which calls or bans the godly into human form or human space. To it belongs the innermost being-seized and being-filled by the appearing, with the whole being, consistently with all senses received godly presence, the construction and impact of the divine in the whole given existence. The divinization of the body is something completely different from the "deification" of the bodily functions; the embodiment of god is equally strong and high, if not a stricter and tougher religion than the world-fiendish."

The sacral basic tone of the sanctification, as an emission of the magic center, has to ring through the whole existence and from this elevated line the last upswing and the darkest crashes have to occur.

One must not believe that these things can be achieved simply with any kind of "practices." They are ultimately a thing of "mercy," that is to say, a thing of the fate. Mercy is not forced by **momentary exertion or schoolmasterly passing of "tasks," but it is a free gift from the gods and itself the sign that in us a god is pushing us to embody him. He who does not have the demonic seed within himself will never give birth to a magical world.**

Nevertheless, something from the god sleeps in every human and could be aroused with the **appropriate fertilization. But not much seed comes up, due to the inappropriate milieu which grows out of the profane benchmarks and tendencies of the mass. The mass of today lives only materially, but not with the body, it feels only intellectually but not with the soul. Even the child is compulsorily subjected to these tendencies (this is called "general education" and "upbringing to a practical life" with the ideal of the "useful member" of human society). One almost has to be a genius today to live such a harmless-sacred life as every sow-herder did in the past.**

The most important means of magical "awakening," besides the general milieu, has always been the contact with an already awakened great one. Just the mere presence in an environment pulsated with a magical stream is enough to let a great deal of seeds blossom out. But for the awakening of the last, the living breath of a great initiated one is necessary and not replaceable by anything. Such breath is already preserved in books.

One should therefore also not believe that one could be able to "learn" magic from this present book, but one can only obtain guiding principles from it, in which oneself and "fate" still have to insert the irrational factor of the "living."

This fertilisation from an individual living great one is one of the rarest occurrences today. But every diffuse living tradition also disappeared, so it is no wonder that the magical existence is in worse shape than ever before. Most are dependent on dabbling on their own account or they fall prey to one of the existing occult "sects," whose leaders also generally have no deeper knowledge and no deeper capabilities. With all these kinds of popular-occultism the possibility to come on a shallow track is enormously reasonable, and one arrives much too easy at the conclusion to consider volatile superficial formations of the psyche and perceptions which are only based on peripheral nerve irritations as magical revelations and wear oneself out in it.

The given directives do not pursue the purpose of supporting such a kind of dilettantism or replacing the incomparable fertilisation by a living master, but they are only designed to establish guidelines for how the development and impact of magical forces has to happen, provided that the necessary above-personal preconditions are present. Such guidelines must never be followed schematically, but they must only serve as an animation, to develop guidelines for oneself from them. In case that certain "exertions" are applied, these must not be considered as "occult experiments" which are performed to "just see if there is anything to it," one should also not consider them as a school assignment which one has to "finish," but they have to pour out of that sacral basic attitude (tenor) that was already indicated. That basic attitude (tenor) is not learned with these practices but these only have a further-pushing value if that attitude is preceding them.

Since the body is the point of origin of all magical effects, our whole attention at first has to be turned to it. This does not mean that we should lock ourselves into an armor of food-, clothing-, and bathing-directions and because of all the details, thereby forget the main point, but that we strive for retrieving what we have lost for a long time: feeling for the bodily and therefore primarily feeling for our own body. Our whole daily life today is resisting any deeper kind of body-feeling and body-exercise, since we are only used to mechanical performances and because of our almost exclusively sitting lifestyle have lost any kind of body-feeling. The common sport and the gymnastics that come along with it provide no equivalent, since the achieved effect is not penetrating into the deep layers of the inner-bodily structure. Recommendable for our purposes is however a certain kind of gymnastics, which we call "sensual" and "articular" and of which we will talk at length later on.

An important point is of course the question of nourishment. It does not rank that high however, as some occultists of today would like to rank it. The body is not a sack, which randomly takes in what you put into it, but it exerts a careful selection and conversion on the given substances, so that it depends first and foremost on the body itself what it wants to keep and what it wants to reject. That there exist nonetheless substances which are taken in by the body submissively and which then act as "poisons" inside of it is well known, and until now no one succeeded in establishing a reliable definition for the term "poison." Technically speaking, every substance which we put into the body is acting as a "poison," that is to say as foreign body. On the other hand, the fasting also has effects which are related to the symptoms of poisoning. Therefore, it has to be classified as an axiom for the whole question of nourishment that we only put those substances into the body whose "effect of poisoning" is in our intention, and that we should keep all those substances away from it which create other kinds of poisoning effects in it. In addition, there is the possibility by abstaining from certain substances, to possibly bring about certain intended phenomena of "self-poisoning," as is the case during complete fasting and during increased vegetarianism.

The whole problem of alcohol and nicotine will consequently resolve itself.

What is put into the body has to be consistent with the intended effect. Vegetarian food is notoriously decreasing the intensity of the animal powers, so that the vegetarian is then easier to control. Man is becoming "tamer." Meat in contrast increases animalism and demands therefore increased efforts for its direction; it makes the man "wilder." The one who only wants intellectual, "bodiless" insight will favour the use of vegetarian food, especially since he is then able to leave aside a whole lot of manipulations and "milieu-instructions." But he will then have to do without the real incarnation of the demonic, because the appearing sensations will always get stuck in the mental. That vegetarianism is advertised so much today is due to the increasing rationality and abstractness of the European man. Since he generally only wants "bodiless insight," vegetarianism is the more convenient for him. But for reaching the higher levels of demonism, this kind of nourishment is definitely not recommended.

He who wants to enter the actual area of demonism and therefore of magic has to be in full possession of all, thus also his animal powers, and will therefore stick to the appropriate meat food. The consumption of meat played a virtually cultic role in the primeval religions, every other kind of food on the other hand was regarded as something almost worthy of contempt. The primitive man still had a sense for the fact that in the meat of the animals, and last but not least of the human itself, a compression of certain world powers is given, which for him reached into mysticism. The content of "mnemonic energy," that is to say of latent memory-substance, and therefore of psychogenic force in general is without a doubt greater with regards to the animal body than the vegetable. He who "eats" an animal is thereby also assimilating the whole ancestral line of the animal, and this one has a greater energetic meaning than the ancestral line of the usual plants which are used for nutritional purposes.

That the consumption of meat principally necessitates much more extensive means and adjustments for the bringing about of magical sensations and actions is connected with the much greater expenses of energies, which come into question with regards to the consumption of meat. Mere thoughts are easy to direct, but as soon as perceptions become real things, whole new problems arise.

What applies to the meat food also applies to the consumption of alcohol, tobacco, and other narcotics. The vegetarian will abstain from them if possible, since they resist its tendencies. They will however some times be much more effective with regard to meat food, due to their affinity. All old peoples knew and used narcotic means and they played an important role especially with regards to the cult and all kinds of magic. J.W. Hauer writes about this: "We know from ethnography that clairvoyance and hallucinations are a frequent effect of certain toxic plants. This shows us that such wonder-acting plants have always been appreciated in some way, be it as juice (like Kawa in Polynesia), be it as powder (like Cohaba in America), be it as intoxicant (like Bhang), or as masticatory (like henbane), laurel, etc. Besides Agnis, wherein the magic fire power is residing, the poison, which is creating the ecstatic excitement, is standing as a coequal companion." The ecstasizing effect of narcotic substances always placed them in close connection to the demon world. Especially the deep symbolism of the process of fermentation has again and again stimulated the fantasy into mystical speculations. Ernst Fuhrmann writes with respect to the portrayal of old Peruvian cults: "The plants and fruit juices which were at all times used to brew intoxicant beverages have been withdrawn from the normal decomposition during the ripening time, and during this time of being-locked-in that peculiar power developed inside the fruit-water, which communicates with the human and creates in him the same fermentation of a great deal of his juices, the ecstasy is there, which then follows a reaction, because the waste from the own juices can not be replaced fast enough. The body falls into a deep sleep, which was stolen from the fruit-material, by rendering the winter-rest impossible. It is this ability for intoxication, which the sun created during the winter time, and that the human now wants to take possession of this creation of the winter, which makes this perfectly understandable to me."

The old peoples regarded meat, blood, and wine as the most precious things which man could ingest, and if he sporadically abstained from them, then this did not happen because of rejection, but to increase his responsiveness towards these substances.

The increasing tendency of abstraction, which equates to the entropic curve of decline of our historic time-ring, did let substitute materials take the place of these archetypal substances, so that meat became bread and the blood became wine and finally water, or at least wine diluted with water, as is the case in the Catholic cult. This "dilution" and this working with "substitute materials" are characteristic of this tendency of the world historical process.

Every culture has its declining part – which, as we have seen, is always the longer one – a tendency for entropy, for dilution, abating, disembodiment, and with it a loss of the gods. What we call "rationalisation" and "mechanisation" is only a form of expression of this tendency, as Ernst Gundolf said: "The so-called mechanisation is the stepping back of the gods out of the time. The gods always live, but not always are they letting themselves into the time." **The magician on the other hand is the distinctly ektropic, that is to say the force-compressing man, he is the custodian of ektropic energy focuses, he acts against all entropic time tendencies and he – and only he – represents**

the point of origin of possible renewals. Hence, the magician always appears antagonistic to the dominating time streams and is therefore always perceived as "evil," but physiologically he appears as atavistic, like every genius. Magic always means a diving back into states, which are "overcome" by the dominating time, that is to say with which the bulk of the time is unable to get on with. Just like the temples and palaces of great epochs have decayed in later times, because the smaller grandchildren were not up to their great ancestors works any more, in the same way are primeval states sinking into oblivion, because the time is "rising above" it, that is to say swimming on the surface. The magician is the man who is always newly able to enter the "status nascendi," and in whom the latent energies are always newly breaking up just like dark memories.

Ernst Gundolf says: "It defines the greatness of a man, how much legacy of the history is again becoming revitalized into reality in him – how great the amount of sleeping and solid substance is, which his being is filling and awakening again, how deep he is reaching down into the sunken layers, to **suck their juices up." Only the magician is therefore able to also learn something from historical symbols, only he is able to interpret life forms which have faded away. Considering what he is learning all contemptuous laughter from contemporaries about the "old" has to become silent. Ernst Furhmann writes** about this: "We have to memorize once and for all that only a priest will get to know something from other priests, and this only in circumstances whose favor are hard to win. Before Europe may have a really new priesthood, it can hardly learn something from other peoples, and it is again this strange tragedy that at the same moment when a new priesthood wants to emerge here and could walk over the earth, the knowledge in the foreign peoples will just have went out."

Therefore, we must always be conscious of the enormous difficulties which are in the way of every magic acting today, we also have to have enough humbleness to not achieve and enforce something which does not depend on our will but on our rank.

The awakening of a new basic attitude towards existence is not the first thing that we must do, but the first thing that must happen in us... Only when this completely irrational, above - moral, and above – personal transformation has taken place inside of us will all instructions given here gain a sense. There is no directive and no rule which could replace this unique act or could be compared with it.

If the fertilisation by a living master is missing, we have to rely on a diffuse self-fertilisation, which requires a high creative potency and includes the necessity of exhausting detours whose traces are never completely obliterated.

Whose fate is leading him to where he is entering - because of his own power or lifted up by a master - the magic level, has reached the stage of the "pupil," and only for him does it serve a purpose to consciously continue the work and observe certain rules and directives.

Only from this point of view does the above given description of the effect of foods, poisons etc. bear a meaning. For the profane man these are merely questions of hygiene, which the doctor has to decide. Also the above indicated gymnastics have only for the real "pupil" more than just a mere sanitary value. No one previously became a magician because of gymnastics and the observation of certain food directives, if not the seed for it had fallen into him from somewhere. But who has the rank or receives it at any merciful moment can increase his powers with such things. Also during the ceremony of certain magical measures certain postures and motions play an important role, just like the ingestion of or abstention from certain substances.

The already mentioned gymnastics have the aim to deepen the body-feeling, to clarify and amplify, but moreover to create certain sensations by practicing motions and assuming certain postures. "Sensual" is how such practices are described, which serve in a smooth manner the increase of the body-feeling, as "articular" on the other hand those postures and motions, which influence the body-feeling by over-bending individual joints. The sensual practices stand for a passive listening-into the body and are therefore preferably happening out of a state of relaxation, the articular practices on the other hand represent a violent, almost mechanical pushing and bending of individual joints or of the whole body. They are happening out of a state of increased tension. If both forms are combined, then certain slinging motions are generated which can be of the more smooth or even the wildest kind. These practices are supported by certain breathing-methods.

The sensual practices are based on us turning off (if possible) all arbitrary motion-impulses and relaxing our body to such an extent that it is still barely standing. At first we assume a position of exhaustion, arms and head are limply hanging down, the body is slumping down and is just about standing on the legs... If we now follow the pull of gravity or act smoothly against it and give it certain counteracting impulses of motion but without giving the movement any kind of aim, then we will notice that our directionless body, because of our will, will create certain vague movements and will automatically assume certain postures. The movements themselves are at first of no interest to us, our main focus of attention must be on the inner-bodily tensions which are thereby occurring. Every movement of our body is initiated and accompanied by certain organic emotions, and in getting used to paying attention to these tensions, they will reach a greater and greater clarity and intensity. The instinctive basis of the indicated motions benefits the spontaneous appearance of such feelings of tensions and lets our body have a say, whereas we are usually always out-screaming the body with our intellectual direction. In this manner, we will newly learn to experience our body, we will realize that it is full of sensations, which until then did escape us completely, and by way of greater and greater empathy, and we will gain the ability to use it for whole new purposes.

In contrast to the tired and casual motions of these sensual gymnastics are the excessive stretching-movements of articular gymnastics. The most important of these movements are those which are concerning the spinal column, because the spine is, as a result of its close connection with the spinal marrow, of outstanding importance for all somnambulant phenomena.

At first, one makes easy trunk-bends to the front, to the back and to the side. Next, one practices trunk circulations on a larger and larger scale. Finally, one kneels on the floor and practices the same things in this position. Hereupon follow the more intense over-bendings of the spinal column. With straightened knees and limply hanging arms, we then bend the upper part of the body forward until the palms of the hand (not only the fingertips) reach the floor. Then one stands with the back in front of a wall, bends the body backwards until the hands reach the wall and now gropes the way downwards while one pushes the back forward. Possibly, one even reaches the floor with the hands, while being backwards, that is to say reaches the "bridge-position," which in many secret orders, like the Rosicrucian Order, had a mystic meaning. The same is practiced with the knees, and similarly the joints of the feet, the hands, and the hip are stretched, too, in order that the body is gaining more and more flexibility. This flexibility exerts an important influence on the overall function of the body, increases the effective potential of inner-body tensions and is, from a purely technical point of view, necessary for the easy execution of certain concentration-postures. The average European would not be able to execute the complicated ones of these positions and to hold them; a simple try would be enough for him to be completely irritated by the occurring pains.

Sensual and articular gymnastics are combined in such a way that one is completely devoting oneself to the occurring motion-tendencies of the sensual practices, and with more and more passionate power is letting them come into effect. Every line of motion is carried out up to the point of its highest excess, and the speed is more and more violently increased, in order that massive slinging-movements, dizziness-movements and abrupt contortions of the overall body or of individual extremities are occurring. One must breathe deeply and, for example, not suppress occurring crying-movements of the throat.

As strange as all this may seem, we have to remember that all of the so-called "acrobatics" of today which can be seen in circuses originated from old cultic practices, and therefore represent occult-magical gymnastics.

As we have seen in the historic part, contortions of the body as well as pathic gestures played a central role in the old magic, and still today the dervishes are "dancing" to bring themselves to ecstasy, and in our churches the enclosure around the most holy is still called a "choir," which is derived from the Greek word for "dance." The presenter in the cathedrals was called leader of the "choralists," that is to say the "dancers." The Jewish Chassidim still dance today on the occasions of their religious celebrations.

Japp Kool writes: "We will more likely come near the truth of the primitive dances and therefore the essence of the dance in general with psychological and religious empathy than with scientific analysis." Robert Blum expresses with regard to the description of hypnotic phenomena: "Rhythmic body movements – dance – are also producing hypnosis." He continues: "Furthermore, narcotics – intoxicating beverages, numbing smokes, etc… may induce hypnosis or states of ecstasy or are at least conducive to it." With regards to our practices, the use of narcotics will also prove itself to be enhancing – and it will be most advantageous if, among other things, real incense is used, which is vaporizing on glowing coals.

The desire for greater care of the body will generally arise on its own while practicing the mentioned gymnastics, and one will learn to understand why washings, baths, embrocations, and unctions have in the past been closely linked to cults and magic. One will also pay attention to the clothes, especially during the practices. The clothes, as the enveloping layer of the body, are of fundamental importance for the whole body-feeling. One will also soon reach the conclusion, that the mentioned exercises are in any case hardly practicable in our usual clothes, and one will automatically drop one piece after the other, until one wears hardly anything anymore. The Egyptian priests were sometimes instructed to be completely naked. Other peoples used a certain "prayer-clothing," which consisted of a lose cloak or cloth.

As soon as one practices the exercises with a naked or sparsely clothed body, the desire for a carpet arises, whereupon one stands and which one also gradually prefers to sit on a chair, since it is an unpleasant feeling to sit upon it with naked skin. Completely without "historicising tendency," one comes therefore back to the cultic objects and certain general ways of life of the old peoples. The Mohameddans still have a "prayer-rug" today, and all old peoples have been more or less "crouch-peoples," that is to say they sat on the floor and not on chairs.

The mentioned gymnastic practices as well as the possible introduction of toxic substances into our body or the keeping away of certain or all foods from the body have the aim to influence our body sphere and in this way change our world of perception. It is a peculiar fact, that we not only exert and receive effects within our world of perception (this is called "empiric"), but that this world of perception can be changed in its basic inventory by shiftings and transformations within an individual object of this world, namely that **object which we call our "body". Our whole world of consciousness is**

most immediately dependent on our body, which means itself only a "thing" within this world, but it is that thing which is the carrier of our consciousness. By influencing our body we change the contents of our consciousness in a much deeper way than by "empirically" affecting these contents (i.e. "things") of consciousness. This gives magic its superiority over all things merely empiric.

To the stated measures now additional practices are coming, which serve the purpose of changing our body sphere and therefore our whole world of consciousness, but which do not reach this effect by centripetal but by centrifugal means, that is to say by means of the central and peripheral nervous system. These are practices which on the one hand work towards the complete destruction of any world of perception, towards an abolishment of any consciousness, that is to say towards "erasing," and on the other hand work towards an immense concentration of the inner-bodily energies in certain points and towards a projection of these energies as plastic imaginations outwards, that is to say as "compressions." Erasing and compression are the axes of all magical practice, and all gymnastic, toxic, and other means eventually only serve the purpose of creating both of these forms of states. Erasing and compression are combined in one notion, in the word of "ecstasy," a notion which therefore contains a double meaning and can be negatively or positively composed. Ecstasy, that is to say "setting beyond" the profane world of perception, is the basis of magic, because only in ecstasy does the person gain contact with his demon, who stands for the source of all magic ability.

The "demon" or "god," as we have seen, is the punctual projection of the whole cosmic and para-cosmic dynamic in us. He is the "cosmos" in its whole infiniteness, but he is also the centre of our "I." He is unapproachable for us on the profane level of the mere "empirical" existence, since our empirical consciousness is not reaching down into these deep layers. He is only approachable for us in "ecstasy," which is stirring up all layers and tearing up the last in order that the empirical is combining with the above-empirical in the "sacrifice." A mild reflection, distant quasi-lightning of ecstasy, is what we have described above as "sanctification." Peryt Shou says: "Every god is the own I in a special cosmic-astral channel, which the I, stimulated by ecstasy to spontaneously view, finds by being reflected in him (the god)." Even to have spent mere moments in this magical state leaves traces behind, which distinguish the pertaining human and his whole world of perception from any other human and his world of perception. Such a human is "sanctified" in the deepest sense of the word. Being a sanctification, ecstasy is not only continuing to have an effect, but is beforehand also having an effect, that is to say magical people are in the state of sanctification often a long time before the actual sanctification happens, and only if this state is accompanying the exertions it is then possible that these lead to the immersion of god into the existence.

The "consecration," the transfer into the state of sanctification by means of ecstasy, in antiquity happened in the so-called "mysteries" at the hand of a master. The natural state of sanctification was always taken for granted, that is to say only humans were admitted who appeared to be "worthy." This natural - pre-existing before ecstasy - state of sanctification was much more frequent in antiquity than today, since the overall milieu was exerting a constant diffuse fertilisation.

"Sanctification" was also called "reincarnation." The old ones already knew that the necessary ecstasy was a free gift from the gods, that is to say is a mercy of fate, and is never enforceable by means of certain "practices." R. Reitzenstein writes about his: "This cannot be taught, only god can awake it in our heart. The process is a begetting, the begetter is gods will; of course, a human father is also acting, who was predestined by this will, and who must himself be reborn, that is to say become the son of god. Because that is the effect of this begetting. The human becomes the all in all just like god and consists himself of the forces of god..."

The whole existence has to be oriented to ecstasy and to unification with the demon, and has to appear as preparation and product of these moments. As R. Reitzenstein also expatiates: "The highlight of religious life is ecstasy, which reaches its most complete and unmistakable form in mystery. If a person is unifying in it with god, he has to hereby gain immediate knowledge, which must be independent of all prior knowledge, and he now talks to god through the servant, who is dedicated to him. The revelation and the immediate view remain also for the priest effect and highlight of the true cult."

We do not possess the, to some extent enormously complicated, means anymore, which the old ones had at their disposal for the consecration. Most notably the most important is generally missing: the master. Here today's man also usually does not possess that sensibility combined with strong animalism, which would be necessary for the demonic act of begetting. In this manner everything remains imperfect piecemeal work, and what we can give here is a number of direction signs to the peaks, which will be climbed only by a very few.

The following exertions must only be practised at night, since it is much more advantageous for the appearing of magical effects than the day. The old mysteries were also always carried out at night and the constellations of the stars, especially of the moon, always received rigorous attention. Robert Blum tried to give explanation for this: "The moon constitutes the negative pole of the heavenly battery of sun, earth, moon, and the electropositive sunrays stream upon that site of the earth which is turned towards the sun, penetrate it and leave as electro-negative at the opposite hemisphere and now stream towards the moon. These negative rays are modified according to the phase of the moon. At night, that is to say on the hemisphere of the earth which is turned towards the moon, the negative streams are causing the nerves to go limp and to only function automatically; the brain is atrophied, the oscillations of the nerve-aether in the ending-neurons are completely stopping, and impressions from the outside physical world can therefore not be transferred to the sense-aether of the soul any more and no feelings are arriving from there at the consciousness." We can therefore understand that the negative nature of night and the moon is benefitting the incidence of ecstatic states, because these demand a "stepping out" of the profane empirical environment.

The first state we try to create is the one of complete "erasure." This erasure is related to the phenomena of the sleep and of the death. Only through annihilation, destruction, decomposition does new existence come into being. The profane so-called "normal" existence must suffer a deep concussion, it must experience such an effective "breakdown" and "de-essentialisation" in order that it is rearranging itself into a new reality. **Omar Al Rashid Beg says: "The world is through fight, life is through annihilation, all construction is through destruction, all emergence is through vanishing – in all becoming lies unbecoming." The state of erasure** can be compared to an illness, as Peryt Shou says: "The soul becomes ill because of the first consecration, because of singings, evocations, postures, similar to a seriotic infection. Through the first initiation did that seriotic poison penetrate into the soul – a poison, which stimulates, excretes and heals."

Since we are lacking the whole cultic machine of the old ones, for the time being we have to be content with a weak reflection of the former mysteries.

One evening with a quiet and concentrated atmosphere, we turn off the light and place a candle somewhere, but dimmed out in such a way that its direct light is not hitting us. We slowly walk up and down the room and breathe deeply. The clothing must nowhere be to restricting. One would be better wearing soft shoes instead of boots. The whole body must be kept very relaxed, the arms hanging down at the sides and the palms somewhat turned to the back, as if one wanted to push air away. The head is slightly raised, as if one were drinking.

We will soon experience that a deep feeling of calmness will gain ground, which will gradually take on a character of numbness. For this, lightly narcotic smoking can be highly recommended.

We give free reign to our thoughts, but are cautious that this reigning of thoughts does not become a "pondering." Daily sorrows must be fiercely repressed and likewise any abstract reflecting is to be avoided.

In this manner the after effects of the daily life are gradually fading away. Now we throttle in a soft manner the thoughts more and more, in order that any kind of imagination is turned off and our inner self is disengaging itself from any conscious movement of the soul. This state of complete emptiness is very hard to reach, because even if we believe ourselves to be completely free of imaginations and thoughts, with detailed attention we will instead observe that this is not the case, that our inner self is continuing to produce imaginations and that we are only pushing them "aside." But the most important point is that we do not create any kind of imaginations anymore.

Now we quietly stroke with the right hand from the head down to the feet, while the left hand is laid upon the back of the head. We are letting the hands sink and wait for what the body is doing on its own. If the aforementioned practices of sensual gymnastics have been successful, that is to say if we are able to let the lightest spontaneous impulse of motion of the body come into effect, then we will experience that our limbs are themselves beginning to move in an undetermined groping way and are remaining in certain, often times hard to find, postures. This is the beginning of so-called "concentration-poses." Larynx and tongue will also begin to move and to form inarticulate syllables. Sound-combinations like "Om-ra", "Am-ara", "Am-an-ara", "Ma-na", "Ur-umbu", "Um-bu", and others will perhaps appear. Movements of the body and syllables will also be linked to one another in a certain way..

The breathing should be calm and even, as in sleep.

We close the eyes, whose lids are beforehand already kept half way lowered. The closed eyes, the calm breathing, and the monotonous mumbling of the syllables must awake the emotion in us, as if we would be more and more plunged into infinite, dark waters, or as if we would be floating in an infinite, empty, lightless room. Here a converging of the closed eyes in the direction of the root of the nose is also beneficial.

During these practices we must not desperately "want", but we must, so to speak, "elicit" the states out of us. The old ones solved this difficulty in the manner that the master brought the pupil into a hypnotic state and then created suggestively the described sensations in him (the pupil). Thus all desperation and convulsiveness of the will on the part of the pupil was impossible. But with regard to the self-fertilization on which we depend most of the time, we have to be, so to speak, master and pupil in one person and the hetero-suggestion must become an autosuggestion, which makes things much more difficult...

During the state of erasure, which we must maintain as long as possible, our living perceptions are sinking back into a "status nascendi," into the energetic original state, which is itself precisely unconscious. Our world of perception is analytically split up and waits for a new synthesis..

Peryt Shou writes about this: "Through autosuggestion we change all contents of imagination into mobile values of the principle of life, the will. The will corrects, arranges, and subjects the contents of imagination. But it is remarkable that the Radsch-Yogi is not forcing the state of autosuggestion, but is letting it happen because of traditionally known causes. Such a state of autosuggestion is at its first level cosmic sleep. This sleep is a return to a state of life of humanity which is stored in the sub-consciousness, and in which humanity created the first mental values, the perceptions... Here we talk about a memorisation, cosmically created in the somnambulant (similar to sleep) universal connectedness, a memorisation about this elementary state of consciousness which goes back to human primeval history..."

The first phase of the ecstatic state has been in former times directly compared with death. R. Reitzenstein writes: "The mystic had to descend into a grave." J.W. Hauer elaborates: "The god of death is in close connection with the consecration; because he is the one who is picking up the seemingly dead person and introducing him into another world. During the consecration Yama, so to speak, pulls the seemingly dead corpse up."

The state of imageless, similar-to-death immersion must cross over into a phase with a more and more strong pictorial nature. This was formerly suggestively brought about by the master, today we have to arrange it ourselves. This is the process of "compression."

We sit or lie down and try – still with the eyes closed – to create the imagination in us, as if we would awake in deep, dark, subterranean caves, on whose ground black waters are spreading. Provided that we possess the necessary predisposition and the first state of erasure was actually reached, now the life of perceptions will rapidly be enflamed. The figures around us, which have a more or less horrible, mollusc-type shape, will automatically compress themselves, and we will perhaps also perceive ourselves in a non-human or pre-human shape. The waters of the deep throw waves and bubbles and exhale foreign damps. And these damps circle around us, agglomerate and elongate, merge and burst into gelatinous masses, enflame in shrouded appearance and sprout heads, limbs, leaves and images of incomprehensible shape similar to the sea-creatures which are neither animal nor plant. Somewhere a dark sun and a dead moon are glowing.

These appearances are not "empty fantasy" but they are projections of very specific energetic configurations in us, are becoming-an-image of the latent cosmic energies in us. These **energies, as we have seen in the theoretical part, have compressed in us, on their way over our ancestors of the human, animal, and mineral kind, and during the state of immersion all these forces float into morphogenesis (becoming-a-shape), that is to say we now view those imageless energies, which are resting in us, as plastic-conscious. Our consciousness wanders through ancient states of existence** of the cosmic in us. That is why very early on this process was described as "transmigration of the soul." The "soul," that is to say the focal point of the consciousness, is wandering, so to speak, through the various structure-stadiums of the cosmic, which are represented by our line of ancestors down to the first star cloud, while our profane life is resting asleep (latent) in us. A.M.O. writes: "Our memory contains a gallery of ancestors which is qualified to evoke knowledge. All our ancestors are interwoven in it. We are therefore able to reawaken the whole history of creation in us." Of course, this reawakening does not apply to the empirical history of creation, so that geology, palaeontology, etc. are discontinued, but it applies to the inner energetic structure of our line of ancestors, which gives a pictorial-energetic morphology of faded-away states of existence. That the emerging images have nonetheless a certain similarity with the empirically verifiable creations of sunken times, is on the one hand attributable to the fact that the empirical is always only the becoming-an-image of certain energetic complexes, and on the other hand attributable to the fact that the fantasy, i.e. the power of imagination, takes possession of such finished formations to fill them by imago-spurious means with contents. It would be in principle thinkable that during a somnambulant immersion in a human of today energy-constellations would awake, as they have been present in the mineral or astral-geologic stadium of our line of ancestors, so that therefore his consciousness would suddenly project the inner-energetic structure of a star cloud or a crystal. For this, his fantasy could also take the empirical image of such a thing and use it for the decoration of the pertaining imagination. A very important role in our line of ancestors plays of course the animal-stadium and therefore appearances of animal-like beings constitute a prominent part. Peryt Shou calls the animals "eternal symbols of wisdom of creation" and further expatiates: "Animals have been especially holy for the Egyptian, since they embodied for him the descending of the godly soul into the substance. The ego has a concealed memory of these – his – evolutionary stages. It releases its concealed treasure. The light of the ancient sun pulls out all the reminiscences as the "membra animae." These stages of development through which the ego has passed and which have been philo-genetically imprinted in the individual are in no way lived out and gone forever."

During this phase the overall character of the occurring imaginations is gloomy, confusing, and horrible. That is why from time immemorial this state was called "descending into hell." The mystic is buried and awakens in hell or the underworld, i.e. the pre-world.

In the theoretical part we have already indicated that all energy is double-sided, and we had identified the ektropic or kinetic side with "evil," the entropic or potential side with the "good." Evil is the dark-violent, irrational, destructive-creative, which eternally appears as inconceivable, unfamiliar and therefore gruesome. It is the principle of Satan. Schelling said about this principle: "Evil is nothing else but the original cause of existence, insofar as it is striving towards actualization in the created being, and is indeed only the higher potency of the cause which is active in the nature." It is therefore understandable, that during the breaking up in the ecstatic immersion, the ektropic focuses of our inner-self at first show images of dread, i.e. hellish visions. The many accounts of "descending into hell" from magic men, and even godly beings (Ishtar, Demeter, Dionysus, Christ, etc.) are an indication that this is not a conceited game, but a psychic experience.

Since the occurring imaginations are coming from cosmic energy-complexes which are lying within our immediate inner sphere of feeling, they are appearing to us not just as empirical "things," but we are experiencing them from inside out as certain projections of the overall cosmic dynamic, that is to say they possess a demonic character for us. Demons differ, as we have seen, from the empiric thing-imaginations in that they appear as certain becoming-an-images of the overall cosmic dynamic, whereas the empiric things are experienced as scattered parts. In the mystical vision the whole appearing "environment" is demonized, that is to say in one moment we view all god-forms or god-images which correspond to the individual stadiums of "our" sunken existence. We view, so to speak, "living mythology". Schelling said about this: "The succeeding gods have indeed taken possession of the consciousness one after the other. Mythology as a history of the gods, thus the actual mythology, could only create itself in actual life, mythology had to be something lived and experienced." The great initiated A.M.O. said: "We call those forces gods, which are worth the trouble of knowing them in such a way. Something can appear as a person (in our sense as "formations"), which is only mental power or a complex of such powers. The god himself does not exist, but is only imagined by us... Forces become formations, if other forces make them into these. If (a) god wants to become a body, he is only able to do it by giving the human an impetus to create him. The god is and is never. What you call god, was never. God is an imagination. But all that we are able to think is an imagination. The power itself is nothing, but only the appearances, and you create these appearances through you and for you. Everything must be introduced into the appearance before it can be recognized."

Therefore, we experience in the magical vision the whole cosmos from the demonic aspect, we view the (in this aspect) acting forces compressed into plastic images, we intuitively become aware of those potencies which form the basis of the creation of every thing-world.

Every history of creation is an interweaving of ektropic and entropic tendencies, which are projected into time and appear as consecutive states. The ektropic moments, the great "acting processes," as Felix Auerbach calls them, are the actual creative, satanic potencies, embodied in Lucifer, whose torch called the great "ignition-phenomenon" of existence into being, the entropic moments, the "elapsing processes" stand for the impact of the induced shiftings of the cosmic-dynamic structure. All birth is a birth from the darkness to the light, from the disorderly to the orderly, from wild to gentle, **from bad to good, from Satan to Seraph. Satan is the beginning, Seraph is the end. Seraph is not "greater" than Satan, he is only the fading-away final act of the hellish thunderstorms of the beginning. But Satan is in everything that lives and appears, he acts in the last tenderest beam of light of the last star, before it is dissolving in the grey twilight of the worlds** of finite entropy. Schelling said about this: "The unruly lies ever in the depths as though it might again break through, and order and form nowhere appear to have been original, but it seems as though what had initially been unruly had been brought to order. This is the incomprehensible basis of reality in things, the irreducible remainder which cannot be resolved into reason by the greatest exertion but **always remains in the depths. Out of this which is unreasonable (irrational), reason in the true sense is born. Without this preceding gloom, creation would have no reality; darkness is its necessary** heritage. The self-conceit of the human is reluctant against this origin out of the darkness (out of "Satan") and he even searches for ethical reasons against it. The effeminate lamentations that in this way the unreasonable would become the root of reason, that the night would become the beginning of the light, rest on the one hand on the misunderstanding of the matter, but they also represent the true system of today's philosophers, who would gladly make fumum ex fulgore (blue smoke from lightning). The revulsion against everything real, which would pollute the spiritual with every contact, must of course also blur the vision for the origin of evil." Jakob Böhme says: "Look, I will tell you a secret, the time has come for the groom to crown his bride; guess where the crown lies? Toward midnight, because the light is clear in the darkness. Everything has bitterness in itself, which is burning, eating it up, and decaying it; this bitterness swells, pushes, and elevates itself into the light and makes the light mobile. A separation developed between the love in the light and the enflamed rage in the darkness. One can not understand the other, but both are **linked together like one body. In everything there is poison and evilness, and it has to be this way, otherwise there would be neither life nor mobility, no color, virtue, emotion, everything would be nothingness. Evil belongs to the formation and the mobility. The bitterness is the root of all things, in it alone there is power and might, the wonders originate from it. The first is the bond of eternity and reaches into the abyss."** William Blake says: "The Giants who formed this world into its sensual existence and now seem to live in it in chains, are in truth the causes of its life and the sources of all activity, but the chains are the cunning of weak and tame minds which have power to resist energy, according to the proverb, the weak in courage is strong in cunning. Thus one portion of being is the Prolific, the other the Devouring: to the devourer it seems as if the producer was in his chains, but it is not so, he only takes portions of existence and fancies that the whole. But the Prolific would cease to be Prolific unless the Devourer, as a sea, received the excess of his delights."

The same process, which is the basis of all that appears, is also intuitively dominating the magical ecstasy. The darkness gives birth to the light and the gruesomeness to the blessedness. The shapes boil, surge, separate, their silhouettes become clearer and freeze to tremendous formations. Darkness still lies on everything and a hellish incandescence. But as the time goes by and we wait viewing, the darkness becomes lighter, the shapes become more subtle and begin to gleam in a light glance. The rocks split and a crystal heaven is vaulting us. The flush of the night and of the steaming deep changes into an emerald brightness, and as if being dissolved in a consuming light we begin to float through circling sun-spaces of blissful entrancement.

The described sensations form the basic experience of the magic ecstasy, the experience of the mystic in the mysteries of the old ones. R. Reitzenstein reports: "At the hand of the high priest the mystic descends into the adyton towards the actual consecration, about which he only reveals that he came to the threshold of the world of the dead and carried by all elements he returned to the light. Out of midnight darkness the gleaming sun illuminated him, he viewed the gods of the world of the dead and of the heaven. The mystery finishes with the beholding of the highest god and the hymn of the mystic, who died and was re-born into the life."

The state after the execution of the mystery or after the magical ecstasy is described as "rebirth," because the man afterwards is not the same as he was before. He has experienced a fundamental transformation, because in him the "god-center," the "demonic center" was opened, so that in a certain sense he now appears as identical with his demon, that is to say he himself appears as "demon" or "god." In any case, he gained demonic powers, i.e. magical abilities. J.W. Hauer remarks about this: "Everywhere where rebirth plays a role with regard to consecration, the opinion prevails that the novice who is in the mother's womb (i.e. in the suggestion-sphere of his master) dies before he is reborn. In his state of death he primarily associates with the ghosts of his tribe, therefore with the "fathers," he also receives a new ghost, oftentimes with a new name, and gifted with the new power he enters the line of those who are able to create new beings." R. Reitzenstein reports: "A mystic, to whom his god appeared, makes a thank-offering and prays: I came together with your holy shape, I acquired strength through your name, I have absorbed your benedictional emissions into me, god, my lord, and now I am allowed to return home in the possession of a godlike nature. The perception prevails, not that the human is elevating himself to be god, but that god is descending into him. A real and definite god emerges, not a somehow deified soul; but to what extent the person is continuing to live in this god is a mystery which the thought is only shyly touching."

For these reasons the mystic was in many places himself worshipped after the consecration. R. Reitzenstein describes this: "As the morning appears, clothed with the heaven-garment and in his right hand the burning torch, on his head the corona out of which ray-like palm branches emerge, the mystic is placed as statue of the sun-god on a pedestal before the goddess and is worshipped as a god by the community." Peryt Shou reports: "The mystic accepted the gesture similar to an arbiter with raised hand and raised forefinger." Schelling expatiates: "Because of the received benediction, the consecrated one became a member of the magical chain, he himself became a Kabir, admitted into the tear-proof context and, as the old inscriptions expressed it, joined the army of the higher gods."

The described magical ecstasy is something very rare and hard to reach. Even great magicians only reached it a few times in their lives. It stands for a becoming-an-image of the para-cosmic forces on a pure hallucinatory or **suggestive basis. This hallucinatory-suggestive process was in antiquity fostered with hallucinatory means, that is to say with a rich scenario, concrete images of gods and concrete ceremonies. We label those empiric objects as "imago-spurious"** upon which demonic inner-complexes can be projected, in order that those objects now appear as embodiment, becoming-an-image of these inner-complexes. All the magic landscapes, demonic appearances and peculiar mysterious events of the ecstasy have been empiric-real, so that the hallucinatory powers of the mystic and the suggestion-energies of the master found enormous support and a positive response **in the empiric environment. The whole cult with its temples and underground vaults, his idols, his sacred groves, gardens, lakes and mountains, his whole magic pomp and solemn ritual was nothing else but a big imago-spurious, a powerful imaginative bastard-creation, which served the purpose to let imageless processes of the inside** become image, become real in the empiric world.

This all is no "outwardness," but a deepening of the real and a realisation of the deep, about which today's materialists, rationalists, empiricists, and ideologists do not have a clue anymore. "Images" are the only thing which we can take in and the godly-demonic is only in the image-form assimilable by us. "A contact can only happen between substance and substance" as Robert Blum says, that is to say between image and image, appearance and appearance.

That sensations, which are occurring during ecstasy, are hallucinatory and suggestively brought about has nothing to do with it, because the same – only in a much milder form – is the case with regards to the "empiric" reality. What we call our "empiric world" is also to a high degree based upon the power of suggestion of our fellow humans, and also the empiric world is "hallucination", i.e. imagination. Carl Vogl says: "Imagination, emotion, deed are in the region of the original experience one and the same. What we traditionally call imagining is a pale, fragmentary replicating of our established perceptual world. The imaginations of the magical "I" are on the contrary approaches, efforts for the formations of another-world. The imagination becomes a hallucination at first for the medium and finally reality, that is to say a complete hallucination for all attendees: it becomes visible, hearable, and tangible, it gets in line with the context of our environment."

We have deliberately portrayed the basic experience of ecstasy in its most complete form, even though we know that only very few of today's living Europeans will actually experience it. But in this manner we gained an idea of the typical sensations, which play a role with regard to pre-forms and de-forms of the great ecstasy.

Even if actual ecstasy is seldom reached, its attenuated forms also grant a deepening of the magical consciousness and an increase of magical powers. This alone is makes it worthwhile to subject oneself to the exertions.

As soon as it succeeds to arbitrarily create the state of erasure and to maintain it for a longer period of time, one can begin with special and arbitrary compression-practices. Here a compression is the plastic clarification and capturing of any kind of imagination. The most suitable object for this is a human, with whom we are bound by any kind of strong emotions – at best passionate love. That such a concentration would be harmful to a still living human (as is sometimes claimed), is a myth. The impact of our concentration always depends on us.

One imagines the pertaining human as pictorial and plastic as possible, but not desperately. One will notice that any desperate effort immediately blurs and disintegrates the image. One must not constantly think "I want, I want," because our will is indeed giving the impetus to the imagination, but this imagination must then be left to its own devices to be able to unfold itself. The only thing our will has to do is to keep other imaginations away. We must totally devote ourselves to the emerging appearance, our whole body must, so to speak, emit it out of its pores, circulate, and nourish it.

The maintaining of the imagined-image must last as long as possible. Hereby we should also try to come into personal contact with the image, speak to it and let it answer, and to communicate with it as if it were an empirical human.

This practice serves the purpose to acquire or increase the ability to compress a certain imagined-image to the highest form and to let it gain continuity. A by-product will often be the phenomenon that the human whom we are imagining by this concentrated means is in the same moment thinking about us, dreaming of us, or is otherwise telepathically coming into contact with us. This phenomenon is sought and extended as an end in itself in pictorial magic, but for the time being we disregard it and foster the imagination per se.

The further practices serve the aim to not only compress the imagination more and more but to also increasingly deepen it, that is to say we try to project complexes of inner forces, which are more and more centrally located, into it. Therewith the appearance of the pertaining imagination also changes, it moves more and more away from the nature-model and gains a more and more mysterious and significant character. This is a similar process as with the artist, who while being in a state of artistic inspiration reforms a natural impression more and more and loads it in this manner with "soul-substance," until the entirety of his inner forces are compressed in the finished artwork. The more central the complexes of inner forces are, the more meaningful appears the artwork and the more it approaches the demonic-sacral world. William Blake for example tells about his artistic work: "I am really drunk with intellectual vision whenever I take a pencil or graver into my hand... The perception of the imaginative eye of every human is as different as the one of the bodily eye and the spiritual mystery unveils itself according to the visionary capacity of the viewer."

With enough intensity of the somnambulant state, the imagined nature-image will gradually gain an almost eerie-holy expression, and the emerging figure is then to be approached as a direct embodiment of an oscillation-form of our demonic inner forces, which have been freed in this manner. This is especially strong if we choose a human as the starting point for the imagination, who already in life also activates our demonic sides. It is not by chance that many of the old masters took their ladylove as a model for their holy pictures.

As soon as one comes into personal contact with such a compressed and deepened imagination, that is to say deals with it as one would with empiric things, one associates with it in the most complete sense of the word.

This demonic association is where we must focus our attention, because our magical powers feed on it. Such an intercourse with demonic imaginations is reported from the lives of all great saints and magicians, and to initiate it, was, as we have seen, the primary purpose of the mysteries of antiquity.

Up until now we have discussed using pure imagination in our exercises. We use imagination for this purpose in an empirical matter; however, imagination alone in most cases will not bring on the desired effect. Again, it is better to visualize actual objects and places. This can obviously be a person, but initially more inanimate objects are preferred because they are simpler and have less detail about them. A flame, a strangely shaped flower, a strange stone, a statue, or any other similar object is more appropriate.

Once you are able to focus on a particular object and have only that object in your mind, it is then that the desire is to increase your ecstasy to the point of body vibrations and ultimately free the consciousness of the body. Nevertheless, we also have learned the hard way that the environment in which you practice is not indifferent, since your mood and environment will have a direct impact on whether or not you have success and how long you can remain detached from the body.

If the imagery exercises were complete and successful it would be possible now to open your eyes and find yourself in the new and different environment.

A careful "imagery technique" therefore belonged to the basic inventory of all ancient religions and magical systems; they found that this practice had a very desirable effect on the body and spirit. It is obvious, however, that their importance is unfortunately falling prey to the progressive trend of abstraction and oblivion.

The best for our purposes as far as a good practicing environment would be a particular room set aside for that purpose only, or at least one corner of our work or sleeping room set aside for our magical conducting exercises. The area should be separated by the use of blankets or rugs. On a small table or above us in hanging style, a candle, or a lamp with colored glass.

You can now either concentrate on the flame or illumination itself to aid in concentration, or choose another object to be placed on the table so that the light falls upon it.

The rest of the room should be completely dark with you only seeing the object or flame.

After some time you should begin to calm and breath evenly and deeply as if you were gone unconscious. Then suddenly, draw a deep breath and hold it as long as possible in the lungs. Do this repeatedly and violently as long as it is bearable. In this way the body becomes more and more heated, there are certain emotional sensations as well which depend on the mood state in which we have at the start of these exercises. If successful it is possible to leave the body consciously or see other entities around us. It is important to keep breathing violently as it has a direct affect on the success of depth of the trance and what is encountered during it. When these sensations have sufficient depth and density, we open the eyes and concentrate our attention on the specific image, i.e. on the flame of the candle or on the image or item. Our entire energy projection unloads now on the flame or image and converts it to our inner demon. It is now the embodiment of the true seat of our inner demonic forces. With this the "external transfer" of the "demon" is now completed and we can operate with the Image as the demon itself with the object in our belief and visualizing becoming the demon.

Again, this is not mere "self-deception", but is strictly an energetic good sense "reality," i.e. the Image is just as the demon, like a house is just a house. "If we see and feel it, it is the only reality" says A.M.O.

All reality is only Phantoms. But even if the reality of this demon image is a "deception" to dismiss – as I said about Buddha – A.M.O. says: "In the beginning was the true demon and I created it to appear to be the deception. False images are necessary for the recognition of truth."

The Image is in a sense, we ourselves - a compression of the entire cosmos. In any case, he is infinitely exalted above our empirical personality, but also above all the other things in our empirical environment.

Understand that this "is" the Image only for ourselves, as any hallucination or manifestation is only for the subject concerned. Nevertheless, all imaginative or broadcasting forces in the purely physical sense, relates to other subjects and can produce similar sensations. These are all based telepathy and visualization.

Reported by M. du Potete are some very interesting facts. He writes: "My effect extended to persons who were at a distance, and those who had been exposed to my thoughts had character changes, or at least changes in the immediate individuality for a brief time. Our thoughts are rays of strange, invisible forces, magical in nature. Once you have given the symbolic character "the Image" its magical power through exercise and belief, there is no need for further preparation of more." You are assured then that even people outside your circle of belief are aware of such image-characters in the strongest manner, and were impressed with the most intense hallucinations.

Items sometimes can influence a magical entity (Images, amulets, etc.), however, that is not our first goal. We must seek only the realization of our "demon" or "God." Everyone has his own particular (item), through his ancestry and his position in the universe "his demon", and he contributes in a very specific, individual projection of psycho-dynamics. This demon has his energy as both forms, as in the differences between the two poles of ektropy and entropy, i.e.: between Satan and God. Robert Blum writes this: "The energy, which can cause changes the visible world, must by necessity be in the two principals of positive and negative together and co exist as one.

These conditions exist in all manifestations of life and the foundation of all evolution." **A.M.O. says: "Your God is both good and evil in appearance and it cannot be otherwise. If your God is not even evil, he is just not God.** God as the almighty should also be all-evil." Schelling said: "The dark nature of his principle is precisely the force which also will be transfigured into light, and both, although only to a certain extent, be one."

Horror always lurks at the bottom of the magical world and everything "holy" is always mixed with horror, as the concept of "taboo" and the "Spirited-saints" is expressed. M. du Potete writes this: "You leave this world through the soul's eye and cannot be fooled. The pleasant visions last only briefly, it will soon be replaced by sudden horrors of ideas suppressed. What is before the eye is nothing more than the drama of life."

Only those self-born magicians and those who feel these forces should enter into the magical worlds of desire. It is a tremendous dream force, an ingenious design of strength, and the freed energies of the universe to be absorbed. If you do not have this power, however, you may do damage to the balance and cause serious injury, which may mean immediate destruction. For this reason, it's the living master, i.e. the magic of genius that is such an irreplaceable factor in magical life.

There are always a few that make the true birth of the demon, the "God," the only thing of importance, but the particular magic of "the people" must be addressed as well. Only when a master magician invokes a "God" and has won the form can the deity enter into life and gain power over the largest complexes of individuals.

Bo Yin Ra says: "Not to look for God anywhere before looking in you. You know not the vital spirit, he should be God above all else and serve the people's needs after he is invoked. Remember that thoughts create the idols and these idols can destroy the faith. Know that these idols are really powerless, but you can endow them with power and not know it! Ahh but still you do not understand that you have power and you've invented idols and mind-gifted them with power through your faith (your imagination). You still do not know that your faith is more than just what you think. Faith in you is the highest strength, remember this, only through faith can we free ourselves from fetters. Through faith we can have all knowledge and realize all dreams. But the key to our deepest faith is ritual and belief and without these we cannot obtain it. "

Once again the birth of the demon arrives, all the other magic in making the closest possible relationship with the demon should be practiced, because everything centers on the magical forces and our demon.

One of the most important endeavors of the old magicians was the exploration of the "name" for demons in question, because the effectiveness of magic is always dependent on certain syllables and formulas based on the demon in question. The most important of these syllables are the names of the demon. The medieval methods to determine the demonic name was based almost entirely on mysterious constructions (conjecture), they were subtle yet scholastic.

Real, however, are other means, which consists of complex symbols corresponding with the alphabet. This means that one focuses on the demon in a casual way, vowels and consonants may come into mind so to speak and give us suggestions and ideas in this matter.

You will then see specific sound combinations like a peculiar sense of "tuning", the "True One's" status and name. It stems from the fact that each set of internal forces with certain positions or movements of the body also corresponds to the voice organs. It is in the same way certain positions and postures give you a rational "sense" to have and possess such syllable combinations and postures. i.e. ancient Jews had their "God's" name in the letter JHVH, the early Christians in the formula JHS.

It is known by most peoples that the magical names of their gods played a tremendous role in their beliefs. Long ago there was demon energy in amounts significant enough to assume certain symbols should be together, however in this time our society "ceremonies" reflect the time when these symbols corresponded to positions and movements of the body, which formerly had occult significance.

Once an image has become a demon and the body has won, all our aspirations must be designed to provide him (in a magic act) to unite with our blood to nourish its magic.

This magical "Communion" with the Deity is the center of magic in every life, it is how we, in the center of all the old cults were... and are today in the Catholic sphere.

In what form the victim ends depends entirely on reaction. Its only principle is that it prefers to create the strongest vibration (shock) and the deepest ecstasy. Very soon you will notice that in specific forms, in particular environment conditions, at certain times, etc. the communal rest is very beneficial and you will use this experience with certain "cult rules" to be creative, not in a superficial way but in a deep physiological manner. All specific religions have known very strict and precisely defined cult rules, and only by the disappearance of religious-magic life and the prevailing ideology of "free recognition" (body free) are we brought this far. Where there is body there is also environment, and this environment wants to be honored, because it comes from the demon.

Each person must find the objects and methods that have the most worrying effect on him and from this build his "victims-technology," i.e. cult rule.

Beyond the direct physiological relationship to the nature of the cult rule, we learn only by regularity i.e. through habit. By understanding this and how habit affects one, one can appreciate the importance of "complex ritual."

The purpose of cult rule is to increase one's imaginative power and when they no longer fulfil this purpose, they must leave, otherwise they become an obstacle. We therefore also notice that lasting reconstruction of cult rules is still evident in all living religions despite their tendency to the conservative.

A true magician will understand and use occult phenomena of all kinds to create, but the first and highest goal is to the divine and to be with his demon.

Only by that life in his demon which protects the magician against the continuously attacking forces, i.e. those cosmic energies attacking his individuality, these forces can be checked and suppressed so that the individual sphere can grow undisturbed.

When you feel the magical powers by the communion with the demon are gathering and growing, you should set certain empirical goals, i.e. profane practical magic.

The first step after this is a focus on the body with the received health and fitness. This focus on health and strength is in the way that it is on the own body sphere, this leads to a deep level of community with the demon and liberated energy. We try to experience our body as effects and as an instrument of the demon. Remember we not only want to be healthy, but we have the idea in us, we are healthy and convert the demonic forces that we use as tools. We must clearly perceive these forces in us. We must never propose that it is all black and white, **but we must always maintain that all suggestive phenomena (imagination) means reality and has a very real impact. "Reality is all that works." All imagination tracks closely with the basic practices of magic.**

As well as on your own body, you can act on third parties and other any items if they are further away. Success is always dependent on the field of concentration and the intensity of ecstasy currently reachable. To aid in concentration, a picture of the other, a garment by him or another item brings us closer with the relevant persons.

First however it is beneficial to refrain from imposing negative effects to others and to restrict oneself to a more diffuse impact of the environment. You should try instead to concentrate on certain individual effects, because you know the natural ways of those forces are still insufficient and contributes only unnecessary and harmful confusion in those forces by astutely maintaining individual targets, instead of a certain power over the cosmic forces as a whole. The cosmic forces lead naturally to the highest achievement of that, allowing the current situation of our destiny lies under a diffuse magical influence. You must want them, yes, but not with obsession at every single stage. Some successes will become apparent at a later time naturally that cannot be achieved at the moment with violent intent.

Similarly it must be understood that magic effects rarely occur in exactly the form and the temporal sequence as you may wish or think. Similar to how the banker will not win an exact certain amount in a specific deal at a specific time but that his transaction will be successful as a whole.

Direct failures you must not fear. **Failures are mountains, they must be exceeded, and often we find the most beautiful places only behind those mountains. We must not be despondent when concerned that the world is against us and the strongest spell remains ineffective. Our demon is struggling, and he is struggling in pain and hardship. We must suffer with him to share victory with him.**

The individual magical special capabilities such as clairvoyance, release of astral bodies, materialization power, psycho-kinesis etc., arise from the specified magic basic facts by themselves. It is always better just to focus the magical-demonical forces on one idea and to set a desirable goal.

For simple clairvoyance, it is enough to achieve a relatively small change in your state of mind. Otherwise, just a light trance state can be initiated by autosuggestion, hypnosis, and through magnetic lines using the Robert Blum radical-dynamic apparatus.

It is only through experience that one can tell the difference between a light hallucination and an act of clairvoyance. The release of astral bodies is only a further special case in these phenomena. The techniques to this act are also independent in part and can be achieved by education and practice. The idea is to intensely and clearly as possible concentrate on a remote location, of the local features, people, etc. to help insure success. You will soon have the experience of actually seeing the people concerned and feel their proximity, which will increase in intensity through visualization.

The philosophy is that true magic is not just education, the magic world should be a learned way of life and means an understanding of our darkest forces and therefore we must undergo a profound transformation.

All true magic is repentance, going back to the time when the deity was still alive, and only when the deity opens its eyes will a magician be able to truly see.

Only the individual who opens the eyes of the deity is given the gift to pass it to others and thus produce new peoples and new circles of being.

The ability to determine circumscribed accomplishments in magical elements (crypto spectroscopy, psychometrics, prophecy, telekinesis, telepathy, etc.) is in all cases due to a special innate talent, often spontaneously gaining insight and understanding of the nature of the universe. It should be understood, however, if one begins with the intent of seriously exercising such individual acts in the study of magic that one would increase the possibility of success and make it much more difficult to get a negative result. The effect of any magic-making depends on the intensity and depth of the target ecstasy, and by increasing such through practice brings one closer to one's own demon. Each force-component, thought, and effort which is not used directly in the production of such ecstasy serves no purpose. So then is the vicious circle that could be leading to disappointment.

Whether or not you choose to exercise and develop any magic ability, it must be said that what abilities are developed are totally dependant on the level of ecstasy you obtain. Also any indiscriminate experimentation of certain phenomena is strongly advised against, curiosity without commitment destroys everything. We should calmly accept the fact that if a serious commitment is not present in these studies disaster could occur both physically and mentally. Those who only come around for the "magic tricks" will never develop any understanding as to its nature.

The first and only important thing is communion with the demon. This act compared to everything else is just a waste of energy, but understand this communion should never be the starting point in study. Any tendency to pursue profane-occult phenomena should therefore initially be avoided. They occur quite naturally as soon as their time has come.

But even if such phenomena do not occur, it is a devotion to the magic, as in this book was written, which gives us a fundamental and crucial understanding for our entire existence. It gives us the gift in a sense to help persuade the hidden gods to make themselves known. Only by doing magic, through practice and gaining experience, will we recognize divinity and learn to be one with her.

This is the goal.

End.